TAROT TIPS

78 Practical Techniques to
Enhance Your Tarot Reading Skills

About the Authors

Ruth Ann and Wald Amberstone are cofounders of The Tarot School in New York City, offering Tarot instruction in several formats and media.

Together the Amberstones teach, write, and publish about Tarot on all levels from divination to psychology to esotericism and magical practice. They are perpetual pioneers of new Tarot techniques, and remain lifelong Tarot students. Between them, Ruth Ann and Wald have amassed more than seventy years of experience as Tarot practitioners. Ruth Ann began her career as a reader in 1974, and Wald began his Tarot studies in 1959.

More than a thousand students have taken live classes at The Tarot School since it opened its doors in 1995. Hundreds more from around the country have participated in Tarot Teleclasses and Telecourses (a pioneering program of classes given entirely on the telephone), and students from all over the world have purchased tapes from The Tarot School Audio Course Series and study The Tarot School Correspondence Course. *Tarot Tips*, the Tarot School's e-mail newsletter, has thousands of subscribers worldwide.

The New York Tarot Festival, presented in June 2002 by Ruth Ann, Wald, and the students of The Tarot School, was the first national and international Tarot symposium to be held on the East Coast. The Readers Studio in April 2003 was the first Tarot conference targeted specifically to advanced students and professional readers.

Special Topics in Tarot

TAROT TIPS

RUTH ANN AMBERSTONE
& WALD AMBERSTONE

with

FOREWORD BY MARY K. GREER

2003
Llewellyn Publications
St. Paul, Minnesota 64383-0383, U.S.A.

FIRST EDITION
First Printing, 2003

Cover art © 2001 by Robert M. Place, background image © 2001 Photodisc
Cover design by Kevin R. Brown
Editing and interior design by Connie Hill

Library of Congress Cataloging-in-Publication Data
Amberstone, Ruth Ann.
    Tarot tips / Ruth Ann Amberstone & Wald Amberstone : with foreword by Mary K. Greer.
       p.   cm. — (Special topics in tarot)
       ISBN 0–7387-0216-1
       1. Tarot—Miscellanea.   I. Amberstone, Wald.   II. Title.   III. Series.

BF1879.T2A475   2003
133.3'337—dc22   2003060580

Llewellyn Publications
A Division of Llewellyn Worldwide, Ltd.
P.O. Box 64383, Dept. 0-7387-0216-1
St. Paul, MN 55164-0383, U.S.A.
http://www.llewellyn.com

Printed in the United States of America

*To our family, friends,
teachers, and students*

Table of Contents

Acknowledgments

We offer our heartfelt love, respect, and gratitude to:

Our students and Tarot enthusiasts around the world for asking the questions that form the basis of this book.

Jo and Norman H. Kass, for their unwavering love and support, which has enabled The Tarot School to exist.

Rachel Eve Brauser, my dearest daughter, for her love and patience with me through the endless deadlines of publishing a weekly newsletter, and the challenges of running my own business.

Lelia Dickerson and Irene Kendall, for helping us envision and start The Tarot School, and for their continued support.

John Rozsa, Ivy Beloff, and the staff of the SLC Conference Center, for providing the perfect place to hold our classes.

David Heizer, for his eagle eye, encouragement, good cheer, and for being our technical lifeline.

Judith Zweiman and Johanna Gargiulo-Sherman, for their enduring friendship and willingness to listen to us talk shop ad nauseam.

Our esteemed colleagues in the Tarot community, from whom we continue to learn and draw inspiration.

Barbara Moore at Llewellyn for her vision, hard work, enthusiasm, and friendship—and for nudging us to write.

Connie Hill, our editor, for all the special magic that editors do to bring this book to the Pentacles stage of creation.

Robert M. Place, for his stunning rendition of the 8 of Pentacles, which graces the cover and captures the spirit of our work.

The beautiful people at SYDA for their Love, Trust, and Truth.

FOREWORD

uth Ann and Wald Amberstone are incredible people in that they have devoted themselves and their lives to the teaching of Tarot to an extent I've rarely before encountered. They've taught their weekly Tarot School class, open to all, in New York City for nine years; they offer a correspondence course with personalized support, teleclasses exploring specialized topics, audiotapes of classes; and they put on the New York Tarot Festival in 2002 and The Reader's Studio in 2003—the first in-depth training for Tarot professionals. More remarkably, they got married at the 2002 Tarot festival, pledging their vows before the Tarot community, in a ceremony filled with Tarot and magical symbolism.

Those who take their correspondence course with the intention of earning a certificate will attest to the high and exacting standards elicited, as well as the the wise and detailed guidance they receive. When attending their class, which I do whenever I am in Manhattan, I am amazed by their powerfully simple techniques that are uniquely different, yet as profound as anything I've yet encountered. Underpinning everything they teach is a deep study of metaphysical and spiritual teaching, of which only a glimmer appears in this book. They are constantly experimenting with Tarot's potentials and expanding their own knowledge about its mysteries.

The practical Tarot tips found here arise not just from a desire to teach, but from a dedication to advancing the student's expertise in and knowledge of Tarot's capabilities, and, even more importantly, from a deep concern that each person achieve an awakening of their own capabilities and an honoring of their own wisdom. These are the ideals the Amberstones consistently impart beneath all their instruction.

Ruth Ann, as is well demonstrated in this book, doesn't try to tell you what to do or think, nor does she present absolutes, but, instead, shares concepts and techniques that have worked well for herself and her friends. Her years of experience and her deep empathy are apparent, yet she always emphasizes the importance of each person's checking to see if the advice fits their own circumstances and worldview. She offers reasonable guidelines, while asking you to trust your intuition.

Why am I telling you so much about Ruth Ann and Wald? It's because I want you to have an experience of this extraordinary couple. Imagine you are attending one of their classes or workshops. Knowing that you have overcome a number of minor crises and annoyances to get here, they've planned for the first experience to be one that will bring you fully into the present and that will awaken your intuitive self. Wald, a smiling figure with a shock of white hair and a round, cerubic face, leads you in a deceptively easy relaxation and focusing exercise. Ruth Ann has an earth-mother presence, with very long, swirling brown hair that is reminiscent of her days as a folksinger. She seamlessly steps in to take you on a short journey to meet a wisdom figure on the Tarot card, chosen to introduce you to the theme of the day. You exit the meditation into a room of fellow-journeyers, the cares and concerns of the outside world left far behind. Wald and Ruth Ann preside like kind but firm parents over this school of wisdom-seekers. Wald generally presents the broad concepts and their philosophical basis; Ruth Ann fills in the details, keeps track of real-world needs, and adds the strength of her practical observations. It is often her exercises and spreads that bring the principles and insights home. *Tarot Tips* is an arena where Ruth Ann excels and her experience prevails, but for anyone who has seen both Amberstones teaching you'll know that it's not easy to separate their individual influences.

There is so much of value in this book, sometimes commonsensical and sometimes unique to their own practices. Don't skip any of it, and don't assume, if something sounds utterly simple, that it won't be the most powerful tool you'll ever learn.

Mary K. Greer
Author of *Tarot for Your Self* and
The Complete Book of Tarot Reversals
August, 2003

INTRODUCTION

The title of this book, *Tarot Tips*, is deceptively simple. In two words, it opens the door on a treasure of accumulated practical wisdom gathered over two lifetimes of involvement with Tarot.

Tarot Tips was begun by Ruth Ann in the fall of 1998 as a free e-mail newsletter that went out to a few of our students and was made available to visitors to the Tarot School website. It was intended to answer simple, direct, practical questions about Tarot reading techniques in a simple, direct, practical manner, and that's exactly what it did. Every week, Ruth Ann discussed things like how to pick a card, how to shuffle a large deck with small hands, and how to choose a first deck from among hundreds of possibilities.

Week followed week, and a year passed. A few subscribers became nearly a thousand, with many from other countries around the world. *Tarot Tips* began responding to reader queries, and as simply and directly as always, answered questions of increasing complexity.

At about this time, I began to help out when Ruth Ann asked me. Saying something practical and useful every week, week after week, began to seem like something that couldn't continue indefinitely, even with the two of us pooling our knowledge.

But another year passed, and with the generous help of some of our colleagues as guest contributors, *Tarot Tips* never missed an issue. The number of subscribers grew to 1,500, and we began to get very sweet letters thanking us for what was seen as valuable work.

A third year came and went, and by the end of it, *Tarot Tips* had become one of the major Tarot newsletters in the world. One hundred fifty issues were in the archives, answering questions and discussing techniques on what would have been, in any other setting, a bewildering array of practical Tarot matters. I hadn't guessed at the beginning that there was so much to talk about.

Eventually, Ruth Ann had the great idea of making *Tarot Tips* into a book, and so a portion of what had been previously available only in electronic form is now between these covers. By no means all the tips that have been written are contained in this volume. *Tarot Tips* remains a work in progress. Its true value is that it is a constantly growing storehouse of the kind of knowledge that everyone needs to be a competent reader. It is pretty fat-free, containing only solid information and well-constructed answers to real questions posed by Tarot students on every level of expertise, from everywhere in the world that Tarot is appreciated and practiced.

It should be noted that, much to our subscribers' general satisfaction, there is not a hint of esotericism to be found anywhere in *Tarot Tips*. I don't mean to say that there are no practical uses described for what is considered to be esoteric material. But the esotericist's perspective and emphasis never gain a foothold. The reader, and the reader's interest, reign supreme.

It is more than a little ironic that it should fall to me to call attention to the absence of esotericism as a virtue, since I am by nature drawn to magic and secrets and the company of those who pursue such things. But it is Ruth Ann's genius for the down-to-earth, and her empathy with the struggles of the apprentice and working reader, that make *Tarot Tips* the small work of art that it is. Everything in it has the effect of making every reader feel comfortable, at home, while constantly learning.

In small pieces, easy to grasp and digest, one technique after another is laid out before you. One question after another is answered. At a leisurely pace, but rather quickly for all that, the small ignorances and awkwardnesses of the apprentice are overcome and disappear. If you are an experienced reader, you will find neat formulations and well-stated answers to difficult questions that you can pass on to your own students. In the process, a considerable portion of the vast practical lore of the Tarot reader is organized and preserved.

The funny thing is that all this happened unselfconsciously. *Tarot Tips* grew one small piece at a time, like a coral reef. Unlike most books, it wasn't written. It happened. And like most organic creations, it works because it is a continuous and appropriate response to a real need. In the world of Tarot literature this is, I think, a rarity. It has been my experience that Tarot books generally have a conscious agenda, perspective, or idea to purvey, or, more frequently, are how-to primers written expressly for a market of Tarot beginners.

Tarot Tips is by no means lacking in ideas, and beginners will find it to be a gold mine of useful information. But what gives it a distinctive, even unique quality, is what it doesn't have, what you won't find in it.

Tarot Tips contains no theory. It espouses no point of view. It advocates no approach. It lays down no rules, not even by implication. It is partisan to no school of thought, and takes sides in no argument.

These remarkable absences might, at first glance, make you wonder what the book does contain, what useful content could survive such an intense distillation. The answer is, in part, that it contains answers to a universe of real-world questions on how to read Tarot. It addresses every practical question about Tarot put to its authors by a large, heterogeneous audience over a period of years. In addition, Ruth Ann and I have raised issues of skill and technique that no one has yet thought to ask about, but which we feel are useful and significant.

Never is any answer or technique presented as absolute or even "right." The one principle we offer as universally applicable is to regard whatever anyone says about Tarot, no matter how expert or authoritative, as a suggestion, only as useful as you find it to be when you actually try it out. If it works for you, use it. If it doesn't, feel free to try something else instead. Ruth Ann and I lay no other claim to knowledge than that of any craftsmen who have learned their craft by long experience.

Creating *Tarot Tips* has been for us, and remains, a labor of love. We hope you enjoy and profit from it as much as we enjoyed writing it. We truly believe you will.

— Wald Amberstone

ONE

DECKS, CARDS &
CARD HANDLING

Questions about Tarot begin when you get your first deck, and sometimes even before that. Do you remember your first deck and how you got it?

You may never have even given Tarot a thought before you received a deck from a friend or relative. Your first feeling when you held the deck in your hand may have ranged anywhere from foreboding to delight, and your first question might well have been, "What's this, and what do I do with it?"

Or maybe you already knew, or at least had heard, about Tarot. Perhaps you had a relative who was a psychic and used Tarot in her work, or you had a friend who had a Tarot deck. If this was your experience, and you found yourself drawn to Tarot, your first questions might have been, "Where can I get my own deck? Which one should I buy?" To complicate matters, you might have heard of the tradition that says you should receive your first deck as a gift. That might have made you wonder if you were even allowed to buy a deck for yourself, or instead, needed to wait for someone to give it to you.

It may be that these early questions are ones you asked recently, or you may have asked them half a lifetime ago. Either way, everyone begins at the very beginning with questions more or less like these. You will also want to know how to acquire a deck, care for it, and handle it; how to evaluate different types of decks among the hundreds, even thousands, that are available; how to choose the one that's right for you; and how to use different kinds of decks for different purposes. We address these and similar questions in this section.

Here, and throughout this book, our answers are given in the form of reasonable guidelines drawn from long experience, rather than rules that you ignore at your peril. They are intended to help you get comfortable with Tarot if you are a beginner, and to be useful if you find yourself answering these questions for others.

Tip #1: The Gift of Tarot

QUESTION:

I bought Tarot cards several years ago, and now someone told me that they must be given to you as a gift! Do you know if that is true? — CH

ANSWER:

No, the "must" part is not true. In some circles, there used to be a tradition that you should receive your first deck as a gift. This is a lovely practice; receiving your first Tarot deck from another reader can add extra personal significance to that deck. However, it certainly is not required. This tradition was started a long time ago when Tarot cards were almost impossible to come by. Usually, at that time, the only way to acquire a deck was to know somebody.

Nowadays, there are hundreds of different Tarot decks easily available through shops, catalogs, and over the Internet. The problem now is only which ones and how many to collect. There are those who still feel that to be properly "initiated" into Tarot, their first deck should be given to them. Even if you choose to uphold this tradition, however, it doesn't apply to subsequent decks you might wish to own.

If you bought your first deck yourself and you like it, by all means use it!

Tip #2: Choosing a New Tarot Deck

QUESTION:

Please tell me how to choose a deck when they are closed up in their boxes at the stores. Do you go by just looking at the outside of the boxes and treat them like crystals (except that you can handle the crystals to feel the energy), choosing the box that speaks to you? — Bonnie

ANSWER:

Even when they're closed up in a box, Tarot decks do have their own personal energy—just like crystals. So holding the deck in your hand and feeling if it is "right" for you is certainly one way to go about choosing a new deck.

However, there are a few alternatives available that can help you make a much more educated choice.

Some stores will have open decks available to look through, so be sure to ask. This will vary from shop to shop, as an opened deck cannot be returned and the extra investment is more than many stores can afford.

We are lucky these days to have access to the Internet. Below is a list of links to sites that feature pictures of hundreds of decks, as well as deck reviews. Together, these should give you a pretty good idea if a deck will appeal to you or not. I've included information about Tarot card publishers, as well. Looking through their catalogs can also give you a sense of the decks that are currently on the market.

Websites

Aeclectic Tarot – http://www.aeclectic.net/tarot/
Sample cards from over 400 decks! This resource site also
features summaries, reviews, Tarot readings, learning resources and forums.

Tarots Lo Scarabeo – http://www.loscarabeo.com
A fantastic catalog of decks ranging from historical to recently
created—beautiful, interesting, and sometimes whimsical.

Tarot.com – http://www.Tarot.com
Choose from over fifty decks and get an online reading (free
and paid readings are available). Comprehensive interpretations accompany the scans.

Tarot Passages – http://www.TarotPassages.com
This "must bookmark" site is updated frequently and contains
up-to-the-minute news on decks, books, and Tarot events.
Includes reviews, scans, and hundreds of links to other useful
resources.

The Tarot Garden – http://www.TarotGarden.com
The Tarot Garden is a commercial site (meaning you can buy
decks here!) that features a searchable database of over 1,000
Tarot and other cartomantic decks, all with good-sized
samples.

Wicce's Tarot Collection – http://www.wicce.com
An excellent site which provides scans of numerous Tarot
decks, deck and book reviews, an exchange listing, and other
information.

Publishers

AGMüller – http://www.TarotWorld.com
AGMüller
Bahnhofstrasse 21
CH-8212 Neuhausen am Rheinfall
Switzerland

Tel. +41 (0)52 674 03 30
Fax +41 (0)52 674 03 40
E-mail: info@agm.ch

Llewellyn Worldwide Ltd. – http://www.llewellyn.com/
Llewellyn Worldwide Ltd.
P.O. Box 64383
St. Paul, MN 55164
Phone: 1-800-The Moon
Fax: (651) 291-1908
E-mail: info@llewellyn.com

U.S. Games Systems, Inc. – http://usgamesinc.com/
U.S. Games Systems, Inc.
179 Ludlow Street
Stamford, CT 06902
Phone: 1-800-544-2637
Fax: (203) 353-8431
E-mail: Catalogs@usgamesinc.com

Also, visit our links page at **http://www.TarotSchool.com/ Links.html** for a selection of sites devoted to individual decks. Many of these sites contain scans of all or most of the cards in that particular deck.

One more tactic you can try is to enter the name of a particular deck into the search engines and see what you come up with.

Tip #3: So Many Decks, So Little Time!

QUESTION:

I have been studying Tarot since December 1998. Until July of this year, I had only one deck, the *Cosmic Tribe,* which I learned by looking at the cards, writing my own interpretation, then comparing with the book. Then, in July, I went on a shopping spree and acquired ten other decks. Now I feel overwhelmed trying to get to know them all.

I have contemplated doing my own comparative study with a new card each week but this seems like it will take forever. I still only do readings with the *Tribe* and would love to branch out. Any suggestions?

Also I just purchased Mary Greer's *Tarot for Your Self* and I subscribe to a couple of tarot lists including Tarot-L, All Things Tarot, and Comparative Tarot. Just looking for the best way to learn— maybe unsub a couple of lists for free time to read more books or spend more direct time with the cards? Thanks for your insights.
— Monica

ANSWER:

First of all, Monica, I'd like to commend you on your enthusiasm! Having a passion for Tarot is a wonderful thing, as I well know, but there's no need to let it get stressful. The study of Tarot can take several lifetimes, so the first thing I would suggest is to just relax and enjoy the journey.

Secondly, just because you own numerous decks doesn't mean you have to read with them all. There are many of us who have great collections of decks and yet only work with two or three on any regular basis. For now, pick a couple of your new decks that call most strongly to you and that complement the energy of the *Cosmic Tribe*. What I mean is that you may find certain decks better suited for certain types of readings or moods. Choose one or two that will lend some diversity to your readings.

While continuing to use *Cosmic Tribe* as your primary deck, begin the practice of choosing a *Card-A-Day* in the morning. If you already do this with *Cosmic Tribe*, switch to a deck you'd like to get to know better. As you go through your day, notice how your personal experiences are reflected in the card. Keep a journal with you to jot notes if you like. At the end of the day, read the interpretation in the book and see how it confirms or augments your own experience.

You can do the exercises in *Tarot For Your Self* with your *Card-A-Day* deck or, if you're feeling ambitious, another deck altogether. The *Tarot School Correspondence Course* is another good source of deep immersion exercises. Although the course works extensively with the symbolism in the *Rider-Waite-Smith/Universal Waite* deck, the techniques can be used with any deck you like.

I also understand that being a Tarot list addict, while being a great way to learn, can be extremely time consuming. My best advice is to subscribe to the digest version of every list you join, learn to scan quickly, and be selective! You can spend your whole life reading everyone else's opinions but it's no substitute for your own hands-on experience.

One last thing. Pick a card from any deck. Find a detail that catches and holds your attention and listen for the message in that detail. Don't worry about what the card "means." When you've done this a few times, you'll have a technique that you can use with any deck—even if you've never seen it before!

Tip #4: Protecting Your Deck

Is there anything wrong with keeping your Tarot cards in their original cardboard box? Not at all—but if you carry them around a lot, the box will start to look pretty ratty and eventually fall apart.

The cards you use (as opposed to the ones you collect) are your personal sacred tools and should be treated as such. Keeping them in a silk or cotton bag, or perhaps a special box, will keep them protected and useful for a long time.

Silk has special qualities that make it an excellent insulator against ambient psychic energy. The reasoning behind this statement is that magical attributes in general are often versions of observed natural qualities. Silk has a very tight weave and is therefore a well-known insulator that doesn't allow heat to pass through it. Extending that quality magically, silk protects against strong ambient energies. Whatever is wrapped inside it will be protected from those energies. Wrapping your cards in silk, or keeping them in a bag that is lined with silk, gives them an extra measure of protection and keeps the energy in your cards clear between readings or meditation sessions.

There are many places you can purchase bags and boxes, or you can make your own.

Tip #5: Cleansing Your Deck

If you receive a used Tarot deck, or your cards are consistently giving you confused impressions, it may be time to cleanse your deck. There are a number of techniques for doing this, including wrapping them in cotton cloth and burying them for awhile in clean soil.

My favorite way of cleansing a deck is to smudge it with incense, preferably sage or sandalwood. Wave the lighted incense over and around your cards in a circular fashion for as long as you feel comfortable. Repeat the smudging once a day for a week, or until you're comfortable with the results.

In between smudgings, place a clear quartz crystal on top of your cards. When you have finishing the smudging cycle, soak the crystal overnight in salt water to cleanse it of any negative energy. If you enjoy ritual activity and would like to make this technique even stronger, you may then leave your deck, with the crystal on top of it, overnight on a window sill in the light of a full moon. You may well experience a noticeable difference in your readings with this deck as a result.

Tip #6: Clearing Your Deck

Before and after doing a reading session, it's advisable to clear the deck. This is done quickly and easily in the following manner:

1. Place your cards in a single, face-down pile.

2. Hold your hands over the deck, palms down and crossed at the wrists.

3. Quickly separate your hands with a forceful gesture.

Clearing your deck in this way will remove any trace of energy from previous readings and prepare your cards for the next reading.

Tip #7: Gentle Shuffling Methods

Shuffling the cards comes naturally to some people, but not to everyone. If your hands are small or the cards are particularly large or round-shaped, you may have difficulty performing the standard shuffling procedure. Also, if your cards are old or especially delicate, you'll want to take extra care when shuffling them. Here are a couple of low impact methods you can try:

1. The Pool
Place all the cards face down on the table in front of you and push them around gently with a swirling motion. Do this in a meditative state, while focusing on your question. When you are finished, you can gather the cards together in a stack again or leave them where they are and choose your cards at random from the pool.

2. Slow-Poke
Keeping the cards in a stack, hold them in one hand. With the index finger of the other hand, poke at the short end of the stack until a few cards stick out the

other side. Pull those cards out and place them on the top or bottom of the deck. Repeat this process, keeping your question in mind, until your intuition tells you to stop.

3. Three by Three

Cut the deck into three stacks. Then cut each stack into three smaller stacks. Reassemble the complete deck by collecting the nine small stacks at random. To complete the process, cut the deck in half, reassemble into a single deck, and then repeat the Three by Three.

Tip #8: Pop-Outs

QUESTION:

I've been wondering about this for a while . . . when a card(s) pops out of the deck while shuffling does it have any significance? — Elesha

ANSWER:

In my opinion, absolutely! Of course, you don't have to take my word for it. If you'd rather ignore them, feel free to do so. There really are no hard-and-fast rules or absolute answers when it comes to technique. It's always a personal choice. You may wish to experiment with this and see if you get any valuable information from these cards.

In general, it has been my experience that anything that happens during the course of doing a reading that calls attention or gives added emphasis to any card should be regarded as potentially useful. There are some instances when reversed cards can be viewed in just this way. Also, cards that keep coming up from one spread to the next fall into this category. The next time a card flies out of the deck, take a peek and make a note of it.

Tip #9: Blank Cards

QUESTION:

The blank card—I use the *Rider-Waite* deck, I am not sure if there are blank cards in other decks. I came across one author who encourages the inclusion of the blank card in the deck. Any insight on this would be very helpful. — Bonnie

ANSWER:

Including the blank card in the deck sounds like an interesting idea. Sort of like the blank rune or a wild card, huh? I've never used the blank card in a reading and am not exactly sure how I'd work with it, but it could be fun to try.

The reason you may find one or two blank cards in a deck is because the entire deck is printed on one large sheet of card stock that's big enough for eighty cards. Since there are only seventy-eight cards in most decks, publishers will often use one of the extra cards to print some sort of information and leave the other one blank.

Personally, we think the blank cards make excellent bookmarks!

Tip #10: Damaged Cards

QUESTION:

Help! My five-year-old slightly tore my Knight of Wands. I have gotten very attached to this deck. Will this affect any of my readings? Will cleansing the deck help preserve "good" energies?

Is it a good practice to have the person you are reading for cut the deck themselves or is it a matter of preference? — Gina

ANSWER:

Before going any further, I'd like to say that, just as with technique, there are no hard-and-fast rules when it comes to the physical Tarot cards themselves and how to handle them.

Over time, you will develop your own set of preferences and rituals based upon your own experience. This is as it should be. Tarot cards are a tool. It is my personal opinion that they should be treated with respect and care but please understand that the magic is within you—not the cards. In fact, with enough study, once you have the cards in your head, you can do perfectly powerful Tarot readings without using physical cards at all.

Although you may personally feel that a deck won't work if it's damaged in any way, I don't think that's true. However, if every time you see the damaged card something inside you tightens up, it could have an effect on your readings because it's having an effect on *you*. Some people would be bothered by it and others wouldn't. You have to get to know your own reactions and sensibilities.

So, let's say you do get upset every time you see that torn card. What can you do?

One thing you may wish to try is contacting the publisher of the deck to see if you can get a replacement card. They may be willing to send you one. It can't hurt to ask.

Here are some other options:

- You can repair the card.

- You can leave it alone.

- You can replace the deck.

- You can buy a second deck to use as a source of spare cards in case any of your other favorites get damaged.

- You can do a healing ritual for the card in question. (Again, energy rituals are a personal choice. If you like them, go for it!)

One way to minimize the risk of damage to your cards is to limit or supervise contact that others have with them. (Of course this doesn't guarantee you won't damage them yourself.)

Whether or not you have a querent handle your cards during the course of a reading is also a personal choice. Having the querent shuffle the cards is a good way to get their energy into the reading, but if this makes you nervous, there are precautions you can take and/or alternatives you can use.

You may request that a querent shuffle the cards in a particularly gentle way as opposed to the standard "casino shuffle." See **Tip #7: Gentle Shuffling Methods** for a couple of low-impact shuffling methods you can suggest. They are also good techniques to use yourself to help prolong the life of your deck and/or if you have small hands.

If you don't want the querent to handle your cards at all (or if you're doing distance readings over the phone or internet), here's how you can still get their energy into the reading:

- Shuffle the cards yourself and ask them to tell you when to stop.

- Ask them how many times they would like you to cut the cards.

- Have them choose a number and count down the cards until you've reached their number. (Reduce large numbers by adding the digits together to arrive at a smaller number.)

- Use a numerological reduction of their birthdate as a starting point for the reading.

Oh—and if your five-year-old is particularly attracted to the Knight of Wands (a card indicating very high energy), you may want to lock them up when you're not using them.

Tip #11: Personal Decks

QUESTION:

Have you seen or used the *Tarot of the Trance,* from U.S. Games Systems? Just wanted to get your take on what has become my favorite deck. I find it difficult to read sometimes for others, but feel it really speaks to me when I read for myself. Is this possible? — Joey

ANSWER:

It's definitely possible to connect with a deck on a personal level and not use it for public readings. It is common practice for many experienced Tarotists to use one or more decks for personal readings and/or meditations that they do not use in any other context. *Tarot of the Trance* seems to serve that function for you and rather than try to force it into service where it doesn't want to go, let this new favorite deck become your private friend and counselor.

Tip #12: Non-Heterosexist Decks

QUESTION:

As a gay male, I find many of the traditional tarot decks to be somewhat heterosexist. Are there gay/lesbian/bi decks available for doing readings for myself and my friends? — Joey

ANSWER:

I feel an answer to this question will be helpful not only to those with an "alternative" sexual orientation, but to all of us who do readings for the general public. Becoming familiar with decks that may be more in tune with the sensibilities of our gay and/or feminist clientele can potentially increase the comfort level of a reading session, thereby making it more productive.

When I asked the late Brian Williams, creator of the *Renaissance Tarot, PoMo Tarot, Minchiate Tarot*, and the *Ship of Fools Tarot* for his recommendations, he offered the following suggestions:

"For a feminist and female-centered view, there are of course *Motherpeace* and Rachel Pollack's *Shining Tribe* tarot. For Tarot decks that encompass a queer male approach, there is Stevee Postman's *Cosmic Tribe*, the late Michael Goepferd's *Light & Shadow*, and, I must say, my own *Renaissance Tarot*. No one of these is expressly or exclusively a gay male deck, but on the other hand all three were created by 'out' gay men and are informed with a queer male (and feminist) aesthetic and world view. Gay men (and others!) seem to relate very well to all three."

One feminist deck Brian didn't mention is *Daughters of the Moon*. This deck has two versions of the Lovers—one with a heterosexual couple, and one with two women (or "womyn"). You might also want to take a look at the *Osho Zen Tarot* which, if I recall correctly, does not really express sexuality one way or another. Even the *Rider-Waite-Smith* deck, except for some obvious cards, was designed with the intent that many of the characters be considered androgynous.

Tip #13: Question-Specific Decks

QUESTION:

Are there particular decks that you (or anyone) have found especially good for certain types of questions? I have a collection of about twenty decks and read mostly with two of them but sometimes intuitively find myself drawn to a different one for a particular query. My main two are the *Hanson-Roberts Tarot* and the *Goddess Tarot* by Kris Waldherr. Lately I've been drawn to the

Shapeshifter Tarot online and to the *Tarot of the Witches* at home.
— Jamie

ANSWER:

I also have quite a collection of decks but mostly read with two—
the *Universal Waite* and *The Healing Tarot* by Rev. Jennifer E.
Moore. However, I will often choose a deck that I feel more closely fits the personality of a querent (once I have a sense of what
that is) or choose one based on the type of question.

For example, when reading for women who have questions
that center around issues of healing or empowerment, I'll use *The
Healing Tarot* or *Daughters of the Moon*. For romantic questions, I
like *Hanson-Roberts, Aquarian,* or maybe *Robin Wood*. For clarity
in decision making, I'll always use the *Universal Waite*. If I'm not
sure, I'll close my eyes and listen for which deck calls out, "Pick
me! Pick me!"

I have no problem using two or three different decks during
the course of a single session. Another time that I'll switch decks is
if I throw a spread that makes no sense to me. That's often an
indication that a different deck would be more appropriate to use.

As far as I know, there are no guidelines that say any certain
deck is best for a particular type of reading. The above examples
are choices that I've made but you're really the best judge of how
you connect with your own decks.

Trust your intuition!

Tip #14: Time for a New Deck?

QUESTION:

I think my deck is the *Aquarian Tarot* and there isn't very much
imagery. Do you think I should buy a new deck? I'm kind of torn
about this because I've had this deck for so long, but I think that it

might be easier if I bought a deck with more imagery. What do you think? — Lizzie

ANSWER:

I have a personal fondness for the *Aquarian* deck. It was the only deck I read with for a very long time. The thing that I like the most about it is how the faces are so mutable. You can look at the same card under different circumstances and the expression will change. They also tend to resemble people you know.

However, you can certainly own and/or work with more than one deck! If you're feeling a need for more imagery at this time, by all means look at other decks to see which ones speak to you. We teach with the *Universal Waite* because all the symbolism and imagery is there and the colors are pleasing and clear. But there are hundreds of decks out there to choose from.

There are several websites that feature pictures of the cards from many decks, and several deck publishers have extensive color catalogues. See **Tip #2: Choosing a New Tarot Dec** for a list of resources. You can also search under "Tarot" at websites such as Amazon.com or at any of the major bookstore sites.

TWO

INTERPRETATION
& MEANING

Before you can do much of anything with a deck of Tarot cards, you need to be able to give at least a modest answer to the question, "What do the cards mean?" And this simple question becomes the focus of a quest for knowledge that can last a long time.

Probably most of the pages of most of the books written about Tarot are dedicated to answering this question. Students of Tarot, even experienced ones, spend most of their time on it, and Tarot teachers give it the bulk of their attention. For new students, memorizing card meanings is usually the first great challenge of learning Tarot.

But often, even more difficult than the task of memorization is the need to find a way to reconcile the many differences, even apparent contradictions, between different sources of knowledge. Teachers and authors abound. Books and decks number in the thousands. Classes can be found everywhere. All of these have Tarot in common, but what they teach is incredibly varied and inconsistent. How is a student, particularly a new student, to find her or his way through this labyrinth? Is there no definitive answer to the question, "What do the cards mean?"

Unfortunately for those of you who like straightforward answers to simple questions, the answer here is "No."

Definitions for the cards depend on variables, such as the different, sometimes even opposed, major traditional systems of interpretation and meaning; the many very different decks and the very different intentions of their creators; and the wide personal differences of approach and opinion that exist between individual authorities.

In this section, we won't even try to tell you what the cards mean. Instead, you'll find well-tested, workable ways of choosing between methods, systems and traditions. You'll also find practical answers to difficult, puzzling, or delicate questions of interpretation and excellent techniques for expanding your knowledge without adding to your confusion.

Tip #15: Getting to Know the Cards

Many Tarot teachers use the *Rider-Waite-Smith* (or *Universal Waite*) deck to teach with because of the wealth of symbolism contained in the cards, the tradition behind them, and the clarity with which they lend themselves to interpretation.

Not everyone likes this deck, however. If you are learning Tarot with this sometimes less-than-favorite deck, there is still a way that you can stay connected with other decks you like better without getting too distracted from your studies.

Many Tarotists enjoy the practice of pulling a *Card-A-Day,* either in the morning or before going to sleep at night. Reserve this special ritual for a deck of your choice. If you like, you can pull the same card from both decks and compare them. This is also an excellent way to get the feel of any new deck you (inevitably) add to your collection!

A way to expand on this practice would be to draw the same card from several favorite or interesting decks. This will give you a feeling for how different images can address the same issue in a given card.

A strong graphic example of what can be gained from this practice would be to compare a card such as XIII–Death in several decks. If you do this, we're sure you'll make some interesting discoveries.

Tip #16: Close Observation

Sherlock Holmes' success as a detective was based largely upon his powers of observation. This is a skill that can be learned and developed. It is a skill that will give you untold benefits as a Tarot reader, too.

An important exercise that we practice at The Tarot School is called *Close Observation*. This is how it works:

Choose a card you'd like to study. Spend a good three to four minutes examining the picture as closely as you can. Memorize every detail. If there are things to count, count them. Notice colors, clothing, posture, facial expressions, etc. Notice where everything is in relation to everything else in the picture. Look at everything; you'll be surprised how many things you've never noticed before, even if you've been reading for years.

But one caution—in this exercise, observe only, and remember what you actually see. Don't interpret anything like mood or attitude or meaning. Do this exercise in complete silence and think of it as an act of awareness and intention. As part of the observation process, close your eyes and see if you can remember the card in detail. Then open your eyes and examine the card again to see if you missed anything.

When you are finished, turn the card face-down and make a written list of everything you can remember. If you are working with a friend, you can take turns saying what you each recall about the card. When you can't remember anything more, turn the card over and see what you've missed.

Simple as it is, this exercise can be thought of as a magical act that has many practical effects:

1. **Objectivization**
   The strict separation of observation from interpretation is the basis of an objective reading. It helps prevent personal projection from entering a reading.

2. **Internalization**
   This exercise will teach you your instrument, the Tarot deck, the same way that typists and pianists know their keyboard. The images of the deck in all their complexity will become part of your mental process. After awhile, you won't even need a deck to do a reading.

3. **Acquisition of Power Objects**
   A power object has inherent magical capacities that a magician can manipulate for his own purpose. Each of the separate parts of a Tarot image becomes a power object by giving the reader access to psychic information separate from the formal meaning of the card. For more information on how this is done, see **Tip #54: A Powerful One-Card Reading.**

4. **Acquisition of a Working Universe of Connected Symbols**
   The separate components of the images that make up the deck are repeated over and over again. Together, repeated visual symbols make meaningful themes and allow you greater scope for interpretation. You'll notice the frequent re-appearance of such creatures as the white horse, the dog, birds, sphinxes; celestial bodies such as suns, moons, stars; esoteric symbols such as yods, pillars, and stone thrones and seats. Each of these is a class of symbol all by itself and has interpretive value as a class.

5. **Magical Doorways**
   In the *Rider-Waite-Smith* deck and some others, each

separate object and action is a key to the invisible esoteric universe that is the source of the imagery in these
decks. The pictures in these cards are a careful construc-
tion of visual bits and pieces that refer, like flash cards, to
specific aspects of that extensive esoteric system. As you
become more familiar with this system, these visual clues
will let you enter and use it in your readings.

If you begin your study of the cards by looking at what's really
there, as compared to what you think it all means, you will have a
sound basis for both interpretation and technique.

Tip #17: Card Meanings

QUESTION:

I am very new to Tarot. In using Joan Bunning's excellent book,
Learning the Tarot, as my starter guide, I'm naturally following it
along with the *Rider-Waite* deck. However, I also have a *Connolly
Tarot* deck, and feel totally comfortable with this one in my hands.
It is the one I'll want to use, at least for the foreseeable future. As a
beginner, how might I relate a *Connolly* spread to the detail given
in Joan's book about *Rider-Waite* card meanings? Some of the
individual cards are given quite different meanings across the two
decks. Surely the cards have either this meaning, or that meaning!
Or is the whole thing totally subjective? — Brian

ANSWER:

In response to your statement, "Surely the cards have either this
meaning, or that meaning," let me quote Rudyard Kipling from
one of his famous *Just So Stories*, "Nay not so, but far otherwise!"

One of the things that confuses many Tarot students is the
seeming contradictions you'll encounter as you read through
books or learn from teachers and/or each other. Does a card mean

this, that, or the other? The main thing to keep in mind is that there are many layers of interpretation to each card—all of them correct and no, not all "totally subjective."

Let's look at some of them:

- **The LWB**
  The "Little White Book" that comes with practically every commercially published Tarot deck is either the first place a person will look for interpretations or the last. Many people either ignore it or go so far as to throw it away. LWBs vary in quality. Some are restatements of standard interpretations that may or may not have anything to do with the cards in the box, and some are written by the deck creator and more in line with the creator's intention. That brings us to . . .

- **Traditional vs. Deck-Specific Systems**
  Many Tarot decks are derivations of established mystical systems and share a common symbolic language. The most familiar of these is the *Rider-Waite-Smith* deck and the numerous decks that use it as a model. The *Crowley Thoth* deck stems from the same esoteric tradition but takes a different approach. There are several decks that use this system as their model. Most of the interpretations you'll find in books have their root in these traditions and are usually transferable from deck to deck.

  In these cases, the more you know of the esoteric symbol systems such as Qabalah, astrology, numerology, alchemy, etc., the more you can add to your storehouse of interpretations. Can you read without them? Yes. However, if you wish to be a really good Tarot reader, you'll want to learn this stuff. Besides, when you know the esoteric attributions for the cards, you'll be able to draw invisible connections that will seem totally magical to your querents.

As more and more modern decks are being created, you'll come across an increasing number of deck-specific systems that call upon a broader universe of general symbolism and are used in very specific ways. I believe Eileen Connolly's deck draws heavily upon Christian mysticism as its foundation, while decks such as Alexandra Genetti's *Wheel of Change* are rooted in a Pagan, earth-centered tradition with touches of popular culture and modern experience. Then there are decks such as the *Faery Wicca Tarot,* where you really need to understand the specific tradition that deck is rooted in to use the cards to best advantage.

You can assign additional meanings of your choice to decks that have their own symbol systems, but it's a good idea to familiarize yourself with the creator's intent first.

- **Personal Intuitive Interpretations**
  The interpretations you come up with based on your own intuitive sense, meditation, and personal experience will most likely be the strongest you have. These will form the backbone of your glossary of meanings. Intuitive interpretations are arrived at through impressions you receive from the pictures on the card and may, or may not, agree with traditional interpretations you find elsewhere.

One thing to keep in mind about personal intuitive interpretations is that they can be especially useful in specific situations. In other words, you may look at a card and get some information from it that is just what you or the querent needs to hear at that moment. The card may never mean that particular thing ever again but that interpretation was perfectly valid at the time of the reading. This type of interpretation is very subjective but that does not diminish its value. You have a tremendous amount of leeway here—there are no rules.

- **Other People's Ideas**

  Interpretations that you pick up from other people will
  tend to be a mixture of the above. You won't really know
  where they got them from unless you ask, and even then
  they may not know or remember. You can pick up these
  additional interpretations from teachers, other readers,
  students in your Tarot class, posts in e-mail discussion
  groups, books, and even automated online readings.

  The number one caveat with other people's ideas is
  to use discrimination. Does a particular meaning ring
  true for you? If it doesn't, just because someone said it
  or wrote it doesn't mean you have to use it. If it interests
  you but you're not sure, write it down and think about
  it.

  One thing that we've discovered as teachers is that
  beginning students often have profound insights and
  fresh perspectives on the cards. So if you're a beginner,
  don't think you always need to take someone else's word
  for it because they've been reading longer than you have.
  If you're a professional, listen to the newbies—you could
  learn something!

  Another great source of other people's interpretations is the querent. Even if the person for whom you're
  reading knows nothing about Tarot, they'll still have an
  instinctual reaction to the picture on the card. This can
  give you some of your most valuable information.

So, how do you apply all this?

How do you know which meaning to use of all the ones you've
collected?

The only answer I have to that is to practice. Keep learning and
trust your intuition. The more you know, the more you'll have
available to you. And the more you practice, the easier it will be to
recognize which interpretation is the right one. A lot of the time
it's obvious.

Here are a few additional points that might help you:

- Which method of interpretation is your strongest? Start with that.

- Which meaning will most quickly answer the question? This is what you want to do, after all.

- What extra bit of knowledge can come in handy?

- What does the *querent* think about the card?

- Which interpretation makes the most sense under the present circumstances?

Don't feel you have to learn everything all at once. Wald and I have been reading for a very long time and we're still discovering new ways to look at the cards—that's one of the things that makes Tarot so much fun! So sit back, relax, and enjoy the process.

Tip #18: Card Meanings and Context

QUESTION:

I have a question regarding how you put together what the Tarot cards mean by themselves with what they mean in a reading. I have been reading Tarot for a few months now. I am studying what the cards mean. However, I cannot seem to figure out how you put what the cards are supposed to mean together with what they mean in a reading situation with a real question. I have an idea, I just need that to be clarified. Thank you. — Lisette

ANSWER:

Your difficulty is one that is shared by many people on different levels. It stems from the idea that the cards have hard-and-fast formal meanings and that readers need to strictly adhere to those meanings in their readings. Actually, those formal meanings are useful only insofar as they are suggestive and helpful to the reader. They are intended to be applied with the variations necessary to make sense in particular situations.

The trick is not to be stiff and formal, but rather to be fluid and graceful in your interpretations. It's something like learning dance steps. There *are* actually formal steps to many dances, but the goal is to interpret and perform them gracefully. Learning to read cards from a book is something like learning to dance from a book. You just have to get in there and do it. If you can, it's a good idea to work with a teacher and practice with other students. There's no substitute for practice—and in practice you'll have to take some chances and stretch those formal meanings into interpretations that fit the circumstances.

One of the best ways to do this is to have a dialogue with the person you are reading for. Be willing to take chances with your intuition and ask for feedback. Use all your life experience and practical common sense, together with the card meanings, to find answers to the querent's questions.

There are many times when you will discover that the message or interpretation that is most appropriate is one that you have intuited from some detail of the image, name or number of the card and has nothing to do with the book meaning at all.

Other people's meanings for the cards, no matter how authoritative, can only be a starting point. Your personal experience is needed to give you a complete vocabulary of interpretations.

The context of the question is always your best guide for choosing which interpretation to use. And if you read each individual card as though you were answering the question with that card alone, you'll begin to see how the cards support each other as a group. The patterns will emerge naturally when the context is consistent.

For more information on how cards can work together, see **Tip #22: Card Combinations.**

Tip #19: Interpretation Systems

QUESTION:

I recently started learning and reading the *Egyptian Tarot*. Since it contained only a small booklet, I started looking on the Internet. I was kind of wondering about all the other Tarot tips that talk about swords, cups and coins. The thing is that my cards do not have these things. So I would like to ask if the reading of my cards really only goes with the direct meaning of these particular cards, or if there is some other kind of system that shows similarity to the other Tarots? I would be glad if you could help me. — Sebastian

ANSWER:

We're not 100 percent sure if we understand your question, but what we think you're asking is whether there is a general system of interpretation that links together decks with widely different images and symbols (including suit names).

There are two parts to the answer:

1. Yes, there certainly are a number of widely held, general traditions of interpretation, each of which can be used with a whole class of decks that have a similar base but different specifics. Generally, these are derivative of the *Waite-Smith* or *Crowley-Harris* decks, some of the European (particularly French) decks, or Wiccan/Pagan, Celtic, and feminist/ethnic decks.

2. There is a whole class of decks that can be described as the personal creations of individual designers. Also, there are attempts by individuals to integrate Greek, Egyptian, Buddhist, Mayan, etc. cultural symbolism into a Tarot framework. There are also theme decks ranging from angels to baseball. These are all widely divergent singular systems that don't really have a common

denominator. I think that your Egyptian deck is one of these. In these cases, you pretty much have to know what the specific deck creator had in mind for his or her deck.

As you become familiar with more and more decks, you'll notice different names for the suits. Sometimes they are very different and will refer to the personal system of the deck creator, but many times they will be variations on a theme. Often, you can use the meanings you have learned to associate with Wands, Cups, Swords, and Pentacles with these cards, even if the names are different.

Here are some variations you may come across:

Wands = Rods, Staves, Spears

Cups = Bowls, Vessels, Cauldrons

Swords = Blades, Daggers, Crystals

Pentacles = Disks (Discs), Coins, Worlds

Ultimately, you are at liberty to integrate any kind of deck into any kind of system you're partial to, but that will be a creative act of your own, and you're on your own when you do it.

As we've mentioned before, the important thing to keep in mind is that whatever interpretations you choose, they should ring true to you. Just because it's written somewhere, an attribution or interpretation will not be useful if you don't believe or understand it. When this happens, take the time to meditate on the card or suit in question and find your own answers. Read other sources and compare them with your personal insights. Learn what you can from teachers you trust and keep expanding your understanding of the symbology and issues of the card.

> *It is through self-knowledge, not through belief in somebody else's words, that a man comes to the eternal reality, in which his being is grounded.*
>
> — J. Krishnamurti

At some point, you'll find what works best for you.

Tip #20: Attributions and Imagery

QUESTION:

I have *The Witches Tarot*. In this deck, Wands represent Air, and Swords represent Fire. To me this seems to be appropriate. However, my friend was looking at my cards last night and said that Wands are supposed to represent Fire, and Swords are supposed to represent Air. Is there a specific Element that each suit represents or is it left to the creator of the Tarot deck?

There was also a difference in our 4 of Cups cards. My card had four people who would seem to represent the welcoming of new friendships or new beginnings, while she said her deck was of a solitary figure. I forget what she said it represented. So how do you learn to read the different cards if there is no set pattern? Just by the cards themselves, and your inner instinct? — LaVonia

ANSWER:

There is a tradition of somewhat over 100 years that links the cards, their names, numbers, and images to an extensive esoteric system. This system includes alchemy, Qabalah, astrology, and other disciplines. Tarot became the one symbolic language that integrated all of these systems. There were a few decks that came directly out of that system and those decks, and the books that explained them, are the basis for all the interpretations of Tarot that came after them.

Of those decks, the most widely known and influential are the *Rider-Waite-Smith* deck and the *Crowley-Harris (Thoth)* decks. These decks are the direct ancestors of the vast majority of decks published in the twentieth century. The card interpretations that go with these decks are the foundation of modern divination with Tarot.

However, Tarot has grown a lot in popularity since the 1960s, and hundreds of new decks have been published since then. Many of these decks represent new traditions in Tarot—for example, Wiccan and feminist systems. These systems, and others like them, often depart from the older ones. The person who creates the deck decides which system they want to follow and designs their deck accordingly. (Some deck creators even create their *own* systems!) The traditional Golden Dawn system, which is the one your friend's deck is based on and the one we use as the basis for our own teaching, associates Wands with Fire and Swords with Air. There are some systems where this is reversed. It's ultimately up to you which one you prefer.

As to the imagery, the pictures in the *RWS* deck and *Crowley-Harris* decks (and others based upon them) do refer to a specific symbol system that can be studied and learned. Most of the more modern decks are strictly artistic interpretations of the creators' personal ideas about Tarot. These decks can really only be read intuitively, and/or by using the interpretations in the book that comes with each deck.

So you have a choice—you can work with the older traditions and learn the rich symbology there, or you can choose a deck for its aesthetic value and use it intuitively. Which is not to say you can't use your intuition with the more standard decks—you certainly can. That gives you the best of both worlds.

Tip #21: Contradictory Interpretations

QUESTION:

I'm fairly new to the Tarot world and I'm baffled by the different interpretations given to the cards by different sources. Sometimes the meanings that I get from a reading using two different decks and interpretations can even be contradictory. Would you shed some light? Thanks. — Ana

ANSWER:

This is a question we have heard many times, Ana, and it's a good argument for getting to know the cards on your own terms and developing your own set of interpretations for them. The interpretations you will find in most Tarot books are a combination of popular traditional meanings and the author's personal take on the cards. Because these interpretations are seen through the eyes of different authors/readers, they may appear to be contradictory from time to time.

The main thing to keep in mind is that each card carries within itself a *full spectrum* of meanings. You can think of it this way: Author A sees one facet of the card, while Author B sees another and Author C sees yet a third facet. From your personal contemplations, you will see a fourth facet of the overall meaning.

So which is right? They all are! The trick is to pick the one that's most appropriate for this particular question at this particular moment. The ability to do that comes with practice.

All these meanings complement each other. Collect them all! Then choose the ones you like best and add them to your own intuitive interpretations. The greater the range of meanings you have for the cards, and the more levels on which you understand them, the deeper your readings will be. I understand that it can be a little overwhelming in the beginning, so just start slowly.

If you choose to use two different decks to answer the same question, or if you repeat the reading a second time using the same deck, consider the second reading to be an elaboration on the first, going more deeply into the issues at hand.

Tip #22: Card Combinations

QUESTION:

One thing that I sometimes get confused about are complicated combinations of cards. I'd like to see a tip on how to go about "telling a story" when you lay the cards out for a reading.
— Jennifer

ANSWER:

Reading card combinations is something that confuses a lot of people. There are a number of techniques that can help you do this. Here are a few suggestions:

- **Get the Big Picture**
  Cards do not have to be next to one another in order to be related. Looking for patterns in the spread is a good place to start.

  1. Take inventory of the suits. How many Wands cards are there? How many Cups, etc.? This will give you a sense of the overall energy of the reading. A spread with a majority of Swords cards, for instance, might indicate a focus on education, communication, mental activity (constructive or difficult), or other topics in the Swords domain. (Learn your suit correspondences!)

  2. Are any suits missing? What does that suggest to you; a problem area, or perhaps an area that's well in hand or irrelevant?

  3. How many Court Cards are there? Do other people play a large part in the story of the reading? Or is the querent looking at things from different perspectives?

  4. How many Majors are there? A majority of Major Arcana cards lends a certain weight/importance to the

reading. The focus here is more on the personal and spiritual evolution of the querent than on day-to-day events.

- **Tell the Story:**
  Place the querent (or yourself, if you're reading your own cards) in the landscape of each card. What is s/he doing there? How does that activity relate to their present circumstance? If you're not sure, *ask!* Move on to the next scene. Do the same thing. Sometimes the "plot" will be sequential, sometimes you'll see "flashbacks" — just as in a movie. Occasionally, there will be subplots. (See **Tip #68: Story Circle** as another way of developing this skill.)

  The most important thing to remember is to keep an open dialogue going with the querent. If, during the course of your conversation, you get new insights about a card you've already covered, it's perfectly okay to go back and elaborate on it.

- **Go with the Flow:**
  Let the story carry you. A lot of times you won't know where the reading is going at the beginning. You'll start with something that occurs to you or seems relevant, and as you speak, more information and insights will come to you. Again, feedback from the querent is helpful in this process.

  The skill here is very akin to conversational skill. Just relax and take it where it goes!

When doing divinatory readings, take a look at the cards that are in close proximity to one another and see if you can find connections between them. Read them as though they were one image that contained all the elements you can see. Whatever additional knowledge you have about the cards can also be considered.

Here are some examples of card combinations with suggestions of how you might interpret them in a reading:

The Magician
In his aspect as an illusionist and master of sleight of hand, the Magician can display great manual dexterity.

Combined with:

- The Chariot: a skilled auto mechanic.

- Ace of Swords: someone who enjoys fencing; a neurosurgeon.

- Three of Swords: a heart surgeon.

The High Priestess
She is the keeper of knowledge and secrets.

Combined with:

- The Two of Pentacles: an accountant, especially at a high level where confidentiality is important.

- The Eight of Cups: a psychotherapist, perhaps specializing in lifestyle changes or twelve-step programs.

- The Lovers: a confidante and/or mediator.

Strength
Physical strength, patience, a love of nature and animals.

Combined with:

- The Four of Swords: the illness, death, or recovery of a pet.

- The Ten of Wands: great physical endurance, combined with patience and good nature.

- The King of Pentacles: a bull market.

Six of Swords
Movement, change of circumstance for the better, journey near or over water.

Combined with:

- The Sun: a move to a warmer climate
- The Hermit: a trip to the mountains, possibly alone
- Eight of Wands: an overseas plane trip or flying to a cruise destination

Six of Wands

Victory, success, an out-of-town visitor, a trip or tour.

Combined with:

- The Ace of Wands: a book-signing tour
- The World: international recognition
- The Eight of Pentacles: a successful sales representative

These are just some ideas to get you thinking. Make your own list of card combinations and see how it adds another dimension to your readings. Have fun!

Tip #23: Difficult Cards

QUESTION:

How do you explain unpleasant cards (like Death, 3 of Swords, 5 of Pentacles, etc.) to a querent? Do you say something up front about not taking the cards literally, do you address whatever concerns the querent may have, if and when such cards come up, or what? — James

ANSWER:

It is a common misconception that there are "good" cards and "bad" cards. Tarot makes no value judgments, and each card contains an entire spectrum of meanings. It is equally possible to find joy in the 10 of Swords and difficulty in the 10 of Cups, for example. The test of your skill as a reader is the ability to go beyond the obvious surface mood of the pictures and to recognize which of the range of possibilities is appropriate at any given time.

It is not necessary to add disclaimers to the cards when they first appear. Just interpret them to the best of your ability as they come up. As long as you, as the reader, are confident and compassionate, the querent will get what they need from the reading.

Keep in mind that very often the querent is already extremely aware of difficult situations in their life and unpleasant interpretations will be appropriate and not unexpected. When this happens, take time to listen. Use the opportunity to help the querent find ways to strengthen themselves and get through the rough time. An ideal goal should be that the querent leave the session feeling better than when they arrived.

Even if you understand the concept that each card contains a full range of meanings, you may still find it difficult to find positive interpretations for some of the darker-looking cards. Here are a few suggestions:

The Tower
The destruction of old structures, while admittedly unpleasant for many, is the fastest route to liberation. Revel in the freedom! The Tower has an explosive energy that can also be an indication of great sex.

3 of Swords
"Three for one and one for all!" Conflicts are resolved through love. The mind is grounded in the heart.

The Devil
Did you know that the esoteric function assigned to the Devil is laughter? Be devil-may-care. The Devil is also a great source of raw power. Tap into it.

10 of Swords: This card talks of endings. An end to suffering; an end to a long-term problem (it took ten years for my divorce to become final!); the dawning of a new era.

5 of Pentacles

Where is the querent in this picture? Perhaps they are behind the stained glass window, inside where it is warm. When this card comes up in a reading it could indicate an opportunity to help others who are less fortunate.

Tip #24: Court Cards

QUESTION:

I have been studying the Court Cards. I often find myself at a loss whether to interpret them as an external person, or a psychological part of the questioner.

1. Any hints on how to work with this?

2. Are these the only two options for interpreting the Court Cards?

Thanks for the help. — Julian

ANSWER:

Court Cards are perhaps the most subtle category of cards within Tarot, but you can learn to use them gracefully and when you do, you'll find a lot of unsuspected power in them. The reason you may have difficulty choosing a particular interpretation for a Court Card is because it is entirely possible for that card to be operating on more than one level at the same time. A single card might address the psychological state of your querent, while at the same time describing someone they know, and simultaneously giving you additional information about the situation at hand. This may sound radical, but you don't always need to choose one interpretation over another. Let's look at some of the options available.

Because the variety of energies contained in the Court Cards are pictured as people, they are most often interpreted as people. Whether a particular Court Card in a spread is understood to be the querent, someone else in the querent's life, or both, depends on context. Where context alone is not enough, your experience and intuition, plus some judicious communication with the querent, should quickly resolve this question. For example, if a woman asks about the outcome of her first date with a man she's just met, the appearance of the Knight of Wands or King of Pentacles is most likely not describing the querent. A young man who has just begun a new job and wants to know how soon he can expect a raise could easily identify with the Page of Pentacles if it came up in a spread about this question. In the case of an emotional disagreement between a mother and daughter, the Queen of Wands might simultaneously describe the rebellious energy of the younger woman attempting to establish her own authority, and the autocratic attitude of the older one.

But a Court Card is not always a stand-in for a person, querent or otherwise. Some other possibilities include:

Timing
Every Court Card has an astrological attribution which can be very useful in determining when an event is likely to happen, or when is the most promising time to begin or end something. Court Card timing can be exact to the season of the year, to the time of an astrological sign, or even to the time of day, down to the hour.

Pace
Each Court Card has a specific energetic quality that can be understood as pace, e.g., instantaneous, rapid, slow, or stationary (cards in the suits of Wands, Swords, Cups, and Pentacles, respectively). This can be a crucial aspect of a reading, and may have little or nothing to do with a particular individual.

Maturity

The rank of a Court Card by itself is often an important clue to the nature of a situation in general. Kings and Queens are both mature and complete, and add their maturity to any situation. Pages and Knights are young and in process, and add their qualities of youth, energy, and unfolding drama to any situation. In the context of maturity, the ranks can refer to particular stages of development such as:

Pages = beginning of a project/venture

Knights = the greatest investment of energy

Queens = the nurturing stage

Kings = completion

Gender

The rank of a Court Card also possesses the qualities of gender. Kings and Knights share a masculine quality that might show itself as logical, direct, goal-oriented, and purposeful. This would be true whether the subject were a man or a woman. Queens and Pages share feminine qualities that might include subtlety, indirectness, flexibility, and patience. These characteristics of gender are admittedly arguable and incomplete, but their direction and general aspect is clear enough, and they also influence any situation in which they find themselves.

Elemental Qualities

Court Cards are compounds of elemental energies. This is among the more esoteric aspects of the Court Card mix, but it is among the most important. Each Court Card is a combination of a rank and a suit, and every rank and suit has an elemental attribution.

The Queen of Pentacles, for example, combines Water, associated with the rank of Queen, and Earth, associated with the suit of Pentacles. The Queen of

Pentacles is known as "Water of Earth," and combines the qualities of these two elements. She would be deliberate, caring, nurturing, and concerned with physical (or practical) and emotional matters. The King of Wands, by contrast, combines Air, associated with the rank of King, and Fire, associated with the suit of Wands. This mixture, called "Air of Fire," would be described as rapid, intense, expansive, and explosive. (You may find different attribution systems elsewhere—use whichever works best for you.)

All Court Cards are expressions of the qualities of these compounds, which are called Elemental Counterchanges. And these qualities qualities strongly affect any spread they find themselves in, whether or not they incarnate as actual people.

To know that all these possibilities for Court Card interpretation exist, and that they present themselves en masse to the reader every time they appear, could be a bit daunting. But they can be learned with a bit of time and patience, like everything else in Tarot. The trick is not to be in a hurry. Use what you learn as you learn it, and keep adding to your knowledge and skill over time.

One more thing. Some of this stuff is easier to find out about than others. You may need to become something of a detective to find out all you want to know. Again, patience and perseverance are the watchwords.

Tip #25: Reversals

QUESTION:

I was wondering about the significance of reading reversed cards. So far, I have disregarded how a card falls, straight or reversed. But I'm not sure if I'm doing the right thing. In both of my Tarot books, there is no mentioning of "reverse," but I bought the *Rider-Waite* deck and the little booklet that comes with it stresses "reversed readings." What is your opinion on that matter? — Aradia

ANSWER:

A lot can be said on the subject of reversals (cards with an upside-down orientation) but here are a few things to consider:

- Reversals can be interpreted as a negative or lessening effect of a card, a delay, a block, or an internal process; something you haven't discussed with other people yet, or something still percolating in your subconscious.

- Sometimes a reversed card is trying to call attention to itself, "Hey, look at me! I'm really important!!"

- Some people don't use reversals at all, preferring to use their intuition to choose the appropriate interpretation from the full spectrum of meanings inherent in each card. (This is also how you would approach a card that's laid out sideways, such as the "Crossing Card" in the Celtic Cross spread.)

- You can be selective about using reversals. Decide at the beginning of the spread if they are appropriate or not. Trust your judgment and stick to your decision.

- You can also be daring and innovative by using a mix-and-match approach. Within the same spread, take each card on an individual basis and decide if you wish to read the reversal or not!

For a much more in-depth look at reading reversed cards, we recommend you pick up a copy of Llewellyn's *The Complete Book of Tarot Reversals* by Mary K. Greer (2001).

Tip #26: Stage Cards

QUESTION:

I recently heard mentioned *Stage* or *Separation* cards. Would you have any information about the stage or separation cards in the *Rider-Waite-Smith* deck. A list of these cards and the reason why they are called "stage" or "separation" cards?

Also are there any other decks with similar peculiarities? — Mary

ANSWER:

In the *Rider-Waite-Smith* deck, there are quite a number of instances where the people in the card are standing on a smooth, flat surface in the foreground. There is a dividing line or separation between this area and the background. Looked at from a certain perspective, the figures can be perceived to be standing on a stage, with the scenery presented on a painted backdrop. Pamela Coleman Smith, the artist who drew the cards, was experienced in theatre and costume design, and that influence is evident in her deck. As far as we know, other decks do not employ this particular design convention.

One really good example of this type of card is the 10 of Cups. Others include the 7 of Swords, Page of Cups, 2 of Pentacles, and the 9 of Wands. One that's not so obvious is the 5 of Pentacles. If you look closely, you can see how the background drapes like a curtain. Go through the deck and see if you spot any others.

A possible way of interpreting "Stage" cards is that what appears to be going on may be an illusion or a fiction. One wonders what's really going on behind-the-scenes. This is certainly not always the case but it bears consideration.

Another way of looking at this, especially in the case of the 10 of Cups, is that the people in the card, through an act of intention, are projecting the image on the backdrop "scrim." In other words, they are envisioning the scene and manifesting it through their will and focused attention. You could also say that what you see in the card is something that the querent is projecting onto the situation. I haven't had much opportunity to verify this theory but it's something to think about.

These are personal interpretations that Wald and I have developed on our own. If there's any official school of thought on stage cards, I'm not aware of it. Most likely, it was originally an artistic design choice more than anything else.

Tip #27: Suits and Creativity

QUESTION:

What suit/element goes with creativity? I see references in books to Wands and Cups. My intuition says it may be both. I feel Wands/Fire provides the initial spark and the action to do something about it. Cups is for incubating and gestating the ideas. Perhaps it's all four elements. I don't know. This is a question I keep going around and around with because I am also an artist. What do you think? How do you view this? — Georgia

ANSWER:

This is actually a favorite subject of mine. As far as Wald and I are concerned, you're absolutely right that all four elements play a part in the creative process.

To finish the line of thinking you began, Swords delineates the steps you must take to execute your project, along with giving you the discrimination necessary to make creative choices along the way. Pentacles gives you the materials and the physical dexterity you need to complete the project and manifest it so that others can enjoy it (more Cups).

So, for example, if we look at all the "elements" that go into producing a painting, you might have something that looks like this:

- the *Talent* to paint (Wands)
- the *Desire* to paint (Wands)
- the *Emotion* to translate that desire into vision (Cups)
- the *Mental Process* involved in translating that vision into an executable plan (Swords)
- the *Paintbrush* (Wands)
- the *Paints*, canvas, palette, easel, apron, etc. (Pentacles)
- the *Training* needed to know how to use the materials (Swords)
- the *Physical Dexterity* to manipulate the brush (Pentacles)
- the *Joy* of painting (Cups)
- the *Discrimination* to make changes along the way and to know when the painting is finished (Swords)
- the *Completed* painting (Pentacles)
- the *Urge to Share* the finished painting with others (Cups)
- the *Pride* in your work (Swords/Cups)
- the *Money* made from selling the painting (Pentacles)

As you can see, all four suits or elements play an integral part in the process. In fact, all four suits are involved in everything! Imagine for a moment what the world would be like if, for example, just the Suit of Wands (Element of Fire) was missing. There would be no light, no heat, and nothing could survive.

You can also classify general types of creativity from the perspective of each of the four suits, keeping in mind that each creative act still involves all the elements in one way or another. These are just some ideas and you may choose to classify them differently:

- **Wands** = painting, writing, conducting
- **Cups** = singing, pottery, flower arranging
- **Swords** = illustration, music composition, computer graphics
- **Pentacles** = dance, sculpture, cooking

Some forms of creativity, such as playing an instrument, are such a tight mix of the suits that it's hard to put them into general categories.

If you do manage to find associations that you're comfortable with, you might find them useful when doing readings involving vocational or avocational counseling.

Or, it could just be a fun creative project!

Tip #28: Suits and Strategic Capability

QUESTION:

Further to your Tarot tip on "Suits and Creativity," I would like to ask whether you can address a slightly similar issue—that is on the association between suits and "strategic capability." I'm not sure if this is a fair question to ask, because strategic traits are rather complex, be it military, business, or organizational strategy.

If I may elaborate a little, strategic capability is a mixture of insight, analytical capabilities, creative thinking, and leadership skills. It involves the ability to define one's mission and vision in an organization, translate broad directions into specific goals and targets, and come up with an operational framework with which one can achieve one's targets within a specific time frame. Not everyone has the ability and not all leaders are good at it. I am just wondering if it is within the scope of the Tarot suits to address something of this complexity? — Peter

ANSWER:

Actually, Tarot is capable of addressing anything, anything at all. Your question concerns just the suits. Let me say first that the scope of your universe of strategy is too small. For example . . .

There is social strategy, which is addressed by the issues contained in Cups. Strategic considerations for Cups would include intrigue—political, social, and familial.

There is a strategy of personal development, the development of talent, skill, and spirit. An example of this would be a talent scout in the old Soviet Union who would go around to every village and hamlet looking for children with the potential to be great at something—athletics, dance, chess, you name it. Having found such budding talent, the full resources of the state were strategically organized to develop that talent to its completion. This is an example of strategy in the realm of Wands.

Another simpler example of Wands strategy can be found in any music teacher into whose care a talented child is placed. The development of the child's skill, understanding, spirit, and discipline is an extended strategic act on the part of the teacher, involving insight, planning, mission, timing, etc.

In the world of Pentacles, of the solid and physical, imagine Michelangelo standing before an untouched block of marble, seeing in it the masterpiece that he would produce from it. In his mind, he would attack the marble in just such a way, in just such an order, with just such tools, and at just such a speed. The masterpiece could not be accomplished without this strategic process.

A more down-to-earth example of strategy in Pentacles can be found in the kitchen of a restaurant. Think of how much planning, precision, organization, leadership and supervision, training, and discipline are required in the operation of a good kitchen.

Strategy in the Suit of Swords speaks for itself. You already mentioned military, business, and organizational strategy. These are the areas that everybody thinks of when they think of strategy. They probably involve strategy on the grandest scale, but, as you can see, the element of strategy can be found everywhere and in everything.

As with all other aspects of the manifest, visible world, it takes a mixture of all the elements in varying proportions to bring something into being. This includes strategy, every kind of strategy.

I say this as a matter of faith because I've seen it work so many times in so many ways, and even where I haven't personally seen specific examples, I can imagine and describe them.

There is a magick for every suit.

There is a humor for every suit.

There is a philosophy for every suit.

The details of strategy in any given case, involving any suit or combination of suits, would be found in the numbers and Court Cards that compose the suit. The more intimate and profound your knowledge of the relationship between the numbers and the suit symbols, the better strategy you could produce.

What exactly are the strategic implications of the Ace of a given suit, for example? I bet you could come up with something if you thought about it. What about the 10s? You can see where I'm going with this.

An arrangement of several cards of different rank and suit organized with a strategic understanding could probably describe any strategic situation. In fact, my guess is that it could predict and manipulate as well as describe.

However, to do this would require a remarkable blend of Tarot and strategic knowledge—which I don't have.

Tip #29: Health Readings

QUESTION:

Are there any books or information about what card has what illness? Health issues are not really spoken of much. I practice Reiki and I am studying the Tarot. I would like to have more knowledge on health issues concerning the Tarot. — Doreen

ANSWER:

The way I've mostly used Tarot for clues on health issues is through the pictorial imagery and sometimes through the esoteric associations with the card. I've only used this system with the *Waite-Smith* deck, but I suppose you could try it with other decks as well. I'd be curious if anyone does that.

Following is a partial list of health issues that may be inferred from the Tarot. It is *extremely important* that you do not use the cards to diagnose for yourself or your clients unless you are licensed to do so!! Seeing any of these symptoms during the course of a reading should only be considered a possible indication of a problem and should always be verified by a doctor or other health practitioner.

That said, here are some examples. Once you've gotten the idea, you should be able to find associations with many other cards as well. This list focuses primarily on physical symptoms and, except in a few instances, does not deal with mental/psychological issues. That is a whole area that I am not qualified to comment on, but which would certainly be interesting to explore.

10 of Swords = Death; acupuncture; internal bleeding; nervous disorder; back surgery; slipped disk; chiropractic; immune system; exhaustion.

2 of Cups = Fertility/infertility; venereal disease.

4 of Cups = Denial; alcoholism; diet; circulation; dehydration.

5 of Cups = Anemia; bad circulation; diarrhea; cold; low red blood cell count; low blood pressure; depression; overindulgence; bulimia; diabetes; poisoning.

8 of Cups = Fungus; insomnia; bloating; sleepwalking; fatigue; withdrawal; autism; missing tooth; leave-taking; drying out.

9 of Cups = Indigestion; gout; indulgence; cravings; cancer; chronic illness; hidden symptoms.

Ace of Wands = Potency; balding; hangnail; problem with thumb; carpal tunnel; osteoarthritis; self-centered; genital warts.

8 of Wands = Adrenal depletion; breathlessness; fertility; ribs; arteries; male sexual (premature ejaculation/too fertile).

9 of Wands = Head injury; shoulder; knee; ankle; jaw (TMJ); bladder meridian.

10 of Wands = Tension (neck & shoulder); headaches; vision; overwork.

King of Wands = Hand; headache; control freak; hip; stroke; wheelchair.

II The High Priestess = Sickle-cell anemia; dehydration; infertility; female; heart; Alzheimer's; amnesia; menstrual; water retention.

VII The Chariot = Paralysis; paraplegia; hardening of arteries; chest.

XII The Hanged Man = Dizziness; metabolism; leg/knee; delusions; immune system.

XV The Devil = Substance abuse; incest; chainsmoking; negative self-image; hemorrhoids.

XIX The Sun = Healthy baby.

And of course . . . **Ace of Pentacles** = Reiki.

Many of these associations came from looking at the actual imagery in the cards and drawing connections between the picture and possible health-related issues.

A good example is the 10 of Swords. The image of a body being pierced by a multitude of sharp objects can easily correspond with acupuncture. The fact that they are arranged neatly in a row along the spine could indicate chiropractic treatment or back surgery, for instance.

As far as I know, there is no written source for this type of association. A broad knowledge of medical conditions and/or therapies will help you recognize the symbolic connections for yourself when you see them. As with all intuitive interpretations, building your own library of meanings is the best way to go.

In addition to the imagery, knowing the esoteric functions and associations will help. For example, the back of the head is connected with the Moon and could be an indicator of vascular tension headaches or other head trauma. The function of sight, which is connected with the Emperor, could indicate vision trouble or blindness. (The esoteric function of sight actually refers to "occult sight," which is a different matter entirely, but, for the purposes of this type of intuitive reading, the more mundane attributions of vision are perfectly appropriate.) There are numerous sources, both in print and on the internet, that offer esoteric associations for the cards. Study them and draw your own conclusions.

Here are two more sets of associations that you can use with the Major Arcana. The first draws upon the traditional astrological correspondences and the second is Qabalistic. You can add these to your personal interpretations.

As with any situation where you have multiple interpretations to choose from, your intuition, along with an open dialogue with the querent, will guide you in the right direction. I'm going to take this opportunity to state again, however, that unless you are a licensed medical practitioner, it is not your job or place to diagnose any illness. These correspondences are merely suggestions and guidelines to further inquiry. They may also prove useful in readings dealing with previously diagnosed conditions.

Astrological Correspondences

Aries = Head, Face; the Emperor

Taurus = Throat, Neck, Ears; the Hierophant

Gemini = Shoulder, Arms, Hands; the Lovers

Cancer = Breasts, Stomach; the Chariot

Leo = Heart, Back; Strength

Virgo = Bowels, Solar Plexus; the Hermit

Libra = Kidney, Loins; Justice

Scorpio = Sexual Organs; Death

Sagittarius = Hips, Thighs; Temperance

Capricorn = Knees, Bones; the Devil

Aquarius = Ankles, Calves; the Star

Pisces = Feet; the Moon

Qabalistic Correspondences

The Fool = Respiratory Organs

The Magician = Cerebral Nervous System

The High Priestess = Lymphatic System

The Empress = Reproductive System

The Emperor = Head, Face

The Hierophant = Shoulders, Arms

The Lovers = Lungs

The Chariot = Stomach

Strength = Heart

The Hermit = Back

Wheel of Fortune = Digestive System

Justice = Liver

The Hanged Man = Organs of Nutrition

Death = Intestines

Temperance = Hips, Thighs

The Devil = Knees, Bones

Tower = Muscular System

The Star = Kidneys, Bladder

The Moon = Legs, Feet

The Sun = Circulatory System

Judgement = Organs of Intelligence

The World = Excretory System

Tip #30: Secret Paths

I'm going to share a secret technique with you. It's one that I have discovered that adds a whole new dimension to your readings. It's called the *Secret Path*.

Essentially, a secret path is a connection between two or more cards. This connection can be obvious or mysterious. You can use this technique in any reading where you would like more information than what is readily apparent. If you really know your deck well and can do this in your head, you can amaze your friends and clients by pulling this information seemingly out of nowhere.

It works like this:

Choose a card (whichever one you like) and find another card in the deck that shares a visual, esoteric, interpretive, or intuitive connection with it. This second card will have an additional or clarifying message to add to the reading.

The Visual Secret Path

Take a good look at the card you have chosen. Notice all the details. What catches your attention? Perhaps it is a design element, a color, or a piece of clothing. (I would tend to discount posture here as too many cards feature characters in similar postures.)

Let's say you choose the 8 of Cups (*Waite-Smith* deck). There is a crescent moon in the sky. You'll also find a crescent moon in the 2 of Swords, the High Priestess, and the Moon cards. Depending upon the subject of the reading, one or more of those cards will have a secret message to impart.

Whatever deck you're using, lay out all seventy-eight cards and look for these visual connections. Make a chart for yourself to help you remember them.

The Esoteric Secret Path

This one requires knowledge of esoteric attributions and correspondences. The more you know, the more you'll be able to use this technique. The trick to finding this type of secret path is to be creative with your associations. One of my favorites is the connection between the Hierophant and the Ace of Wands.

The Hebrew letter associated with the Hierophant is *Vav*, which means "Nail." There are also three nails protruding from the top of his crown. Is there another card that has this type of

nail? If you look closely, you'll find one holding up the top penta-
cle in the 8 of Pentacles (Universal Waite). Also, the Ace of Wands
features a very prominent thumbnail! You can take the secret
path of either the 8 of Pentacles or the Ace of Wands for more
information.

Or perhaps you could take it in another direction: nail rhymes
with snail. This takes you straight to the 9 of Pentacles. (You don't
remember the snail in the 9 of Pentacles? Go look.)

Besides the Hebrew letters, esoteric secret paths can be found
through astrological attributions, shared sephiroth on the Tree of
Life, numerology/gematria, esoteric functions, titles, intelligences,
etc. Again, the more you know, the more powerful this technique
becomes.

The Interpretive Secret Path

Here you'll be working with the meanings of the cards. If, for
instance, you associate the Death card with transition or transfor-
mation, which other cards suggest a similar theme? The 8 of Cups
comes to mind for me, as does Judgement. If I were looking at the
terminal aspect of Death, I would be drawn to the 10 of Swords or
one of the other 10s instead.

Trust your instincts here. All the cards have many layers of
meanings and each of us has come to our own understandings.
You may find the choices a little overwhelming at first but just
relax and don't try too hard. Go with whatever comes to mind
first.

The Intuitive Secret Path

This secret path is the most personal one. The connection is purely intuitive and can be made for any reason whatsoever. It may
even be that the second card will just come to you without a formal connection at all. To develop this technique, practice choos-

ing a card in your mind rather than physically drawing it from the deck. Then interpret it, looking at the card if you need to. You might not think that a mental draw is as accurate or random as doing it with the actual cards, but trust me, it works just fine.

The Reversed Major Secret Path

The next time a Major Arcana card comes up reversed, take a look at its numerological partner. You may find the information you need is found there:

21–The World / 3–The Empress

20–Judgement / 2–The High Priestess

19–The Sun / 10–The Wheel of Fortune

18–The Moon / 9–The Hermit

17–The Star / 8–Strength

16–The Tower / 7–The Chariot

15–The Devil / 6–The Lovers

14–Temperance / 5–The Hierophant

13–Death / 4–The Emperor

12–The Hanged Man / 3–The Empress

11–Justice / 2–The High Priestess

10–The Wheel of Fortune / 1–The Magician

This technique is very playful, and the play is to find connections. There is no right or wrong way to go about it, and no rules as to when to use it. I wish you many joyful discoveries as you explore the secret paths of Tarot!

READING TECHNIQUES

In the flow of a Tarot reading, the individual cards are filled with meaning. They are the boats that carry us comfortably and safely downstream. Spreads connect the cards into the meaningful currents of a reading's themes and issues. It is the unending task of a student of Tarot to accumulate an ever more complete knowledge of these things in order to constantly improve as a reader. Happily, this knowledge is available in orderly systems that can be systematically learned.

But to negotiate the unexpected hazards of a reading— the shallows, rapids, rocks, and falls—a reader needs a set of skills rather than a body of knowledge, one that is by its nature a bit unruly, disorganized, even chaotic. This skill set is called by the deceptively simple name "Reading Technique."

What do you do when you look at a perfectly familiar card in a reading, only to go suddenly and completely blank about what it means?

How do you stay objective, and therefore useful, when doing a reading for someone you know very well (including yourself)?

What do you say to a querent when your gut instinct disagrees with the clear meaning of the card you are reading?

These and a thousand other intractable questions have been answered, and answered differently, again and again by readers over the years. They are the answers born of experience, validated by experience and not by theory. They can be told by someone who knows to someone who asks, but every reader has to personally test and personally validate the answers all over again. Reading technique is always learned in the doing.

There's a lot to learn. Just as there is pretty much a bottomless well of meanings and interpretations, and hundreds if not thousands of spreads, there is a very large and growing body of recorded technique. We know this can be a pretty daunting realization. So much to learn, so little time. But here, as in all big projects, things tend to go step by step. Everyone, from beginner to expert, adds to their knowledge little bit by little bit, but progress is still remarkably quick as long as you keep learning.

In this chapter, you will find our answers to a number of real, very practical questions asked by our students. By their nature, our answers cannot be definitive, but you will find them helpful. We have also included other things we think you would like to know and will be able to put to good use.

Tip #31: Expectations

QUESTION:

Why is it with most Tarot readings the message you get is so watered down, and it's so long that by the time you've finished reading it, maybe you have gotten only one or two things from it? It seems so many readers tell you the same thing several different ways, so you think you're getting an in-depth reading, and really you're not.

Also, why do the readings focus so much on things you already know, instead of more on what you don't know? Like your future?

It ends up being more of a counseling session. I think most people really want the emphasis to be on the future than on guidance. Just my opinion. Would love to hear yours. — Lorraine

ANSWER:

You raise an interesting issue that would probably elicit different responses from different people. I can only speak from my own point of view. Your question really covers two separate concerns.

The first, regarding watered-down messages, is strictly a matter of skill. A skilled professional reader should listen carefully to your questions, clarify your questions to find out what you *really* want to know, and make sure those questions are answered to the best of their ability. (It's amazing how many people forget to do this!) This process should include an ongoing dialog to make sure you are getting what you need from the session and to address any additional questions that may come up during the course of the reading.

As to your frustration at not being told the future, we are of the strong opinion that if straight prediction is what you're looking for, you should find and consult a psychic reader. It has been our experience that the Tarot is at its most useful and reliable when used as a tool for guidance, but that's because it's what we do best. The cards themselves do not have powers—these come from the reader. It may or may not come as a surprise, but Tarot readers are not all alike. Every reader has a different talent and a different predilection, and does the kind of reading at which they're best.

If you have certain requirements and expectations of a reader, you may wish to speak to them *beforehand* and discuss their approach. This will help you make an informed decision and go a long way toward reducing the level of frustration for both of you.

Tip #32: Asking a Question

QUESTION:

I've just recently picked up on the Tarot (even though I've had my cards for two years—go figure) but I'm not certain how you would start a reading. Does the querent tell you the question they are asking, or should they expect to keep that to themselves? Should they tell you more about the situation, or do I leave that all up to the reading? I've been trying some practice readings on my family with both, and I find that the reading is more accurate when they do tell me. Either way I was just looking for your opinion or some advice would be appreciated. — River

ANSWER:

I agree that a reading will be much more productive if the querent asks a question. The more background information they can give you as well, the deeper you can go and the more targeted and useful the reading session will be. Granted, there are many readers who actually prefer to work without a question, but that's a matter of personal style.

Some background information should be discussed as part of the process of clarifying the question. Other things may occur to the querent only after the reading has gotten under way. Also, some people will be more forthcoming than others. Be sensitive to what is comfortable for your querent.

In my opinion, the question is one of the most important parts of the reading and the reading can only be as clear as the question asked. If the question asked is ambiguous, the results will often be less than satisfactory. Helping the querent to define and refine their question will save time and ultimately be much more useful.

Learning how to pose productive and targeted questions takes time and practice. Here are some suggestions:

- Think of the initial question as an onion—what questions lie beneath the original question?

- Is there a more specific way the question can be worded?

- Has the querent asked what she or he *really* wants to know, or is there a hidden or buried issue?

Another technique to is to take a lead from the popular American television show *Jeopardy.* This is a game show where the contestant is given the answer and then must guess the correct question. Instead of having the querent ask the question, try backing into your reading by first asking the querent, "What answer would you like the cards to give you?" and then define questions that will yield this answer. For instance, "I want the cards to tell me that the book I am writing will be a success." Some questions based on this answer might be:

- What can I do to make sure I finish writing it?

- Will I make my deadline?

- Is there a market for my book?

- Is my agent the right person to promote it?

- What is my definition of success?

Design your spread to answer the questions that arise.

Of course, this technique is no guarantee that the cards will always tell you what you want to hear. If the writer of this book has no talent, contacts, or drive, the answer could very well be disappointing—but by asking the right questions, at least they'll know why. The information uncovered in the reading should be useful enough to help the querent come to terms with or overcome the difficulties.

Tip #33: Clarifying the Question

QUESTION:

I did a Celtic Cross for a dear friend on a very critical matter regarding his career. He is in the midst of a discrimination case, going on for two years.

> On positions 7, 8, 9 and 10: Judgement, Justice, 7 of
> Wands and 9 of Cups

This was very promising. A week later, I found out that he lost his case. I was baffled because this has never happened before; what actually occurred was the exact opposite of what the reading seemed to predict, although, I found out that if he can get two people to support his claim for racial discrimination, he still has a chance. This twist was not a previous consideration.

I really feel I let someone down, with the help of Tarot. The question was simple: "Will my efforts to fight for what I believe is right be decided in my favor?"

He is out his lawyer's fees and part-time employment. This person gives up a lot to fight for a cause (he's an activist). He had hoped that his case would be a precedent, a deterrent to ongoing discrimination and harassment in the workplace. — Bonnie

ANSWER:

You did not let him down—and neither did the Tarot.

Tarot took the long view. It is very responsive to questions *as asked*. Apparently, his "efforts to fight for what he believes is right" are not over. Therefore, the outcome has not become final yet. You said he still has a chance if he can find a couple of people to back him up. He now needs to decide if he has the strength and resources to see his fight through to the end.

Also, since he is an activist, that fight is probably lifelong and encompasses much more than this particular case. In the long run, those efforts will be rewarded but that may not help him now.

And, because he is an activist, chances are pretty good that he had already made up his mind to pursue this matter and was looking to the Tarot for confirmation. Don't feel that you talked him into anything he didn't want to do. This is his agenda, not yours.

Just a technical note: if you want to know the outcome of a specific event (i.e., trial or case), the question should focus on that specific event.

If your friend wants to consider an appeal, and agrees to let you read for him again, refine the question as much as you can. Ask multiple targeted questions about the case, the witnesses, the judge, his chances of winning this case, and anything else he might need to know to help him.

Oh, and don't use the Celtic Cross if you can possibly help it. That spread is fine for general readings, but what you want to do here is create a spread that will answer the specific questions you need answered. Take the time to work out a list of what he really needs to know so that the answers are useful.

Tip #34: Ten Practical Questions to Ask the Tarot

I can't stress enough how one of the most important components of a successful reading is the question and how it's asked. The more targeted a question is, the more likely it is the answer will be useful.

I really dislike the term "proactive," but it aptly describes the type of question that will yield the best results. Here are ten examples that you can use singly or in combination:

1. What do I need to know about . . . ?

2. What is the next step I need to take to achieve . . . ?

3. What can I do to help . . . ?

4. What is standing in the way of my . . . ?

5. How can I best overcome the obstacle of . . . ?

6. How can I be a better . . . ?

7. Which is the best choice between . . . ?

8. What can I do to support myself while . . . ?

9. When is the best time to . . . ?

10. Who am I?

Question #9 requires some knowledge of timing techniques in order to best answer it. (See **Tip #42: Timing in a Reading**.)

Question #10 is not so easy to answer but I wanted to include it because as far as we're concerned, it's the most important question you can ask the cards. Finding the answer is a lifelong process of discovery, and the more you study Tarot, the better you'll be able to answer it.

Happy readings!

Tip #35: Quiet Querents

QUESTION:

How do you handle a person who doesn't interact with you or want to tell you their question because their feeling is the cards should tell you what's going on? — Susan

ANSWER:

Many people who consult readers do so from the conviction that the cards have a power of their own, and a good reader is in tune with that power. For querents like these, the ordinary talents of perceptiveness, card knowledge, empathy, and compassion are irrelevant. All that counts is the psychic miracle, and if a reader cannot produce, or at least appear to produce this miracle, the querent will feel cheated. It is best for both querent and reader in such a case to be up front about what the reader is and is not prepared to do.

Of course, there are many readers who actually *prefer* that the querent not ask any questions or say anything until after the reading. Such readers have learned the trick of rapidly discovering a querent's issues and interpreting the cards around those issues. This is a special technique and can be learned, like everything else. The psychic approach will appeal to some readers more than others.

To get the most out of a reading session, I personally believe questions should be clarified as much as possible and a meaningful dialogue carried on throughout the reading. I make it clear to the querent before I begin that this is how I read. I tell them that the more specific they can be, the deeper we can go and the more helpful the reading will be to them. If the occasion warrants it, I also explain that I am not here to "put on a show."

The analogy of doctor and patient comes to mind here. Imagine a patient who refuses to tell the doctor what's wrong on the grounds that the doctor, if he's any good, should be able to figure it out. That always seemed to me like a great waste of valuable time.

Even so, there may be times when the querent genuinely does not have a specific question. At times like this, you can suggest drawing a card to answer the question, "What does _____ need to know right now?" Oftentimes, this can act as a conversation starter. If not, you can then go on to draw several cards in a particular category such as health, work, love, etc.

Sometimes, people will refuse to ask a question out of fear. They really do have a very serious question but are afraid to voice it. They hope that the cards will give them the answer they need without having to say anything. Unfortunately, you have no way of knowing if this is what's going on. The only thing I can suggest here is to do your best to pay attention to your querent's energy and/or body language for signals of tension or anxiety and to read with compassion as much as possible.

Another instance when you might encounter the "quiet querent" is mid-reading. If the person you are reading for becomes tired, distracted or withdrawn, you can re-establish the interaction by giving them something to do.

A favorite technique of mine is to offer the querent a card and have them study it for a minute. Then ask them how it makes them feel when they look at it and/or what it brings to mind. This is also an excellent technique to use if you momentarily lose your focus or concentration—or if you suddenly find you have nothing to say about a particular card.

Tip #36: Paying Attention!

I think the one lesson I have learned is that there is no substitute for paying attention.
— Diane Sawyer

This is certainly a valuable lesson to keep in mind for life in general but is especially important to remember when you are doing a reading for another person. There are four things in particular to pay attention to:

1. The Querent

2. The Question

3. The Conversation

4. The Close

- **The Querent**
Take some time to really observe the person you are reading for. Make sure they are comfortable and have everything they need before the reading begins, such as water or tea, a pen and paper for notes, etc. Attention to creature comforts, both the querent's and your own, will start a reading off on the right foot.

  During the reading, watch their body language. Sometimes physical reactions can give you feedback on your reading even if they don't say anything. Watch their energy level and endeavor to keep them relaxed and engaged in the process wherever possible. *Observe.*

- **The Question**
This is the focal point of the reading. Take time to examine the question and clarify it so that it best reflects what the querent really wants to know. Many times a question will have underlying questions that can be more important than the one that was first asked.

  Once you have determined what the real question is, make sure you answer it. This may sound obvious but it's easier than you think to get sidetracked by other issues and forget to give a solid answer to the initial question. *Remember.*

- **The Conversation**
Be very attentive to everything the querent says. As a teacher, I have the unique opportunity to oversee live readings performed by other people. I can't tell you how many times I've observed the querent casually throw out a crucial piece of information that was missed because

the reader was too preoccupied with what they were
going to say next and wasn't paying attention. *Listen.*

- **The Close**
  Whenever possible, the querent should leave the reading
  feeling upbeat and optimistic—or at least with a plan of
  action to help them in the direction they need to go. If
  this isn't the case, take the time to draw one more card
  which will tell them what to do next. I like to close by
  saying "I hope this has been helpful." *Ask for feedback.*

Of course, paying attention to what is in the cards is equally
important. Just because you've seen a card 100 times before,
doesn't mean you won't see something new this time if you pay
attention!

Tip #37: Ten Ways to Pick a Card

One of the first steps in beginning any reading is picking a card to
start with. Whether you are doing a one-card reading or an elaborate spread, you need to start somewhere. Here are ten suggestions to get you started:

1. **Off the Top**
   The simplest way is to shuffle the deck and start dealing
   the cards off the top of the deck.

2. **Cut to the Chase**
   Another easy method is to cut the deck in half and draw
   cards from the top of the bottom half.

3. **Piling it On**
   Cut the deck into multiple piles, depending upon the
   spread you have chosen. For a three-card spread, for
   example, cut the deck into three piles and draw a card
   off the top of each pile for each of the positions.

4. The Fan

Spread the entire deck out in front of you in an arc or fan shape. Hold your hand slightly above the cards and run it back and forth. When your hand gets warm or you feel a little tingle, stop and choose the card under it. Repeat this process as often as needed.

5. Go Fish

Swirl the cards around on the table into a "pool." Choose the card or cards that catch your eye.

6. Play the Numbers

Pick a number and count down from the top. For instance, if the number is 7, you'll start the reading with the 7th card. This is a good method to use when the person you are reading for is not physically present, as in a phone reading, since it puts some of their personal energy into the layout process.

You can also incorporate a little numerology into your reading, based on the number that's chosen.

7. Hot Date

A variation on the number theme is to use the number that corresponds with the date the reading is being done. Or, to personalize the energy even more, use the date of your querent's birthday. If their birthday is on March 4, for example, you would count down either four cards (for the fourth) or seven cards (three for the month and four for the day). If they're willing to give you the year of their birth as well, do a quick numerological reduction of their whole birth date. That's best if the information is available. If you're reading for yourself, of course, use your own birth date. This is another good method to use when the person you are reading for is not present.

8. Double Date
If you're doing a relationship spread, you'll want the energies of both parties in the reading. First, count down from the top of the deck for Person A and choose their card or cards. Then count up from the bottom of the deck for Person B, using their birth date.

9. The Name of the Game
Another way of personalizing the starting point is to use initials. If the name of the querent is Esmeralda, for instance, count down *A-B-C-D-E* to the fifth card and start there.

10. On the Fly
Shuffle the cards until one flies out of the deck.

Tip #38: Deck Orientation

QUESTION:

If you flip cards or turn them over does it matter how the client hands you the deck? If they slide the deck to you, do you turn the deck around? If they turn the deck around and hand it to you, do you leave it as is? Is the answer just be consistent? — Susan

ANSWER:

If you choose to read reversals (upside-down or flipped cards), it is best to maintain the orientation of the querent's shuffle. So if they're sitting across from you and they slide the deck toward you or hand it to you, you should turn the deck around before drawing the cards. If the querent turns the deck around first, leave it that way.

Also, when you turn the cards over, be careful to turn them sideways as opposed to flipping them end-to-end. This will also preserve the correct orientation of the cards.

If you do not work with reversals, it doesn't matter how you receive them as you'll orient the cards as you lay them out.

Tip #39: Going With Your Gut

QUESTION:

If you look at a Tarot Card and you get a feeling from the picture that is opposite from what the book or basic meaning of the card is, should you go with your gut feeling or the book meaning of the card? — Jill

ANSWER:

There are two schools of thought on this, Jill, but as far as we're concerned, your intuition, or gut feeling, is what's ultimately most important.

When reading with Tarot cards, the cards themselves serve two functions. The first is to provide a focus for any natural psychic or intuitive ability you have. The second is to give you a vocabulary of interpretations and symbols to help you express your impressions.

This vocabulary comes from several sources. There are many Tarotists and book authors who have taken the time to write out and publish their own interpretations. Read as many of these as you like, but understand that no one author has the definitive word on the meaning of a card. Find which meanings work best for you.

There are symbol dictionaries that are an excellent resource for adding to your understanding of particular pictorial elements. There will be times when a detail in the card will hold the message. That message will most likely have nothing to do with any standard interpretation of the card.

There are also highly developed symbolic systems such as Qabalah and the magickal systems of orders such as the Golden Dawn. Learning as much as you can of the esoteric symbology of the cards adds even more to the resources you have at your disposal.

The main thing is to be flexible, learn as much as you can, and trust yourself. And don't forget to communicate with the querent! If you aren't sure if your interpretation is the most appropriate one, ask. Dialogue and feedback are just as important as anything else.

Tip #40: Drawing a Blank

It happens to the best of us; you're in the middle of doing a reading for someone, everything's going along very nicely and suddenly it happens—you turn over a card and can't think of a single thing to say. All the interpretations you've ever learned about that card have simply disappeared into thin air!

It can be a gut-wrenching experience when this happens, but it doesn't have to be. There's a simple technique you can always rely on to get you back on track. Pick up the card and put it in front of the querent. Then ask them to look carefully at the card and tell you how it makes them feel. Don't ask them what they think it might *mean*—focus on the emotions that the card elicits.

Use their response as a springboard to further discussion about that card in particular, or how those feelings relate to other cards in the spread. In the unlikely case that both of you draw a blank and have no response to the card, you can always say, "We'll come back to this one later." Sometimes, cards that are read later in the spread will offer the insight you need to interpret it.

Tip #41: Reading Numbers

QUESTION:

I am fairly new to Tarot and I have been receiving your *Tarot Tips* for about a month, and I think they are great. Thanks so much for sending them. It is so good to know that I am not the only one who has such questions. Keep up the good work.

I just listened to your radio interview and I thought it was great to finally put a voice with those tips. It was a great interview and very interesting. One question I do have is that Wald asked about numbers before reading a card. Could you tell me a bit more about reading numbers and where I could maybe learn more about it? Thank you! — Kimberly

ANSWER:

I use a very simple numerology. It concerns itself mostly with styles of energy that tradition associates with the various numbers from 1–10. Since there are many systems by which these numbers can be interpreted, and since they all have useful things to say, if you want to use numbers for interpretation, build a personal system that you can be comfortable with. Such a system is usually a mix-and-match sort of affair.

Everybody knows some of this stuff. A lot of it is intuitive. The rest can be found in a variety of books. The main source for the kind of interpretations that I do is the numerology based on the Qabalistic Tree of Life. You can find a useful short form of that in *The Tarot School Correspondence Course* and in Robert Wang's *Qabalistic Tarot*.

In addition to the numbers themselves, it is useful to realize that when a person chooses from a set of graduated possibilities, like a series of numbers, that choice is usually connected intuitively with the chooser's state of mind. This is what gives accuracy and validity to any interpretation of a chosen number, regardless of the system used.

So, for example, if a person chooses the number 9 out of a group of 10, that person gives us a quick look at the state of their energy with regard to whatever question they ask. The simplest thing that the number 9 suggests is coming to the end of a process—approaching a stage of completion.

If the same person asks a second question and chooses, say, the number 1, you could at the very least safely assume that, in this case, the person was at the beginning of things rather than at the end.

Tip #42: Timing in a Reading

There are many approaches to reading Tarot but as soon as the question of timing comes up, you are using the cards as a predictive tool. Predictive readings can be tricky, and many Tarot readers are reluctant to do them, but I'm going to go out on a limb here and tell you that I believe they have their place. I have come across several methods of seeing time frames that I particularly like.

When it comes to timing, trusting your intuition can work but this is where card knowledge can be especially helpful. Approaches for predicting timing vary from simple to complex. Here are a few systems you can apply without too much trouble.

Take a look at the numbers on the cards. Are there multiples of any particular number? This can be a good clue. For example, if two or more "3" cards show up, you're looking at the possibility of three hours, three days, three weeks, or three months. (Making predictions in terms of years is really stretching it and I wouldn't trust them!) This is where your intuition and the context of the reading may suggest the best time frame to choose.

Another good indicator of time can be found by looking at the suits. Again, see if there is any one suit that is represented in the majority of cards. Then use the time of day or season attributed to that suit to help answer your question of timing.

Swords = Morning and Spring

Wands = Noon and Summer

Cups = Evening and Autumn

Pentacles = Midnight and Winter

You may come across different attributions elsewhere but these are the ones that we use.

The suits can also give you a sense of how quickly or slowly things may move. The energy of the masculine suits of Wands and Swords is faster than that of the feminine suits of Cups and Pentacles, with Wands being the fastest and Pentacles the slowest. We have used the following associations with a great deal of success:

Wands = Days

Swords = Weeks

Cups = Months

Pentacles = A year or more

One more timing technique that I find useful is to lay cards out in a calendar spread, looking for the first card that is most representative of an answer to the question.

For example: a common question asked is "Do you see a relationship coming up for me in the future, and if so, when?"

After having the querent shuffle the deck, draw one card per month until you reach a card that might indicate a relationship. It could be the Lovers, the 2 of Cups, the 9 of Cups (often seen as the "wish card"), any of the Knights, the Ace of Cups, etc. Use your intuition and you'll know it when you see it.

So if you were doing this reading now, the first card would represent the current month. If the 2 of Cups was the fifth card laid out, the chances would be best for a relationship in five months from now. You can also look at the cards leading up to that time to see what kinds of things should be worked on in the meantime.

I do not recommend going any further than one year into the future. It sometimes happens that none of the twelve cards laid out are appropriate. That could mean that either the event in question will not happen during the course of this year or that this is not the right time to ask. When this happens, take a look at the cards to shed light on what else is going on instead.

If you are familiar with the astrological associations of the cards, you can use those to give you a sense of timing as well. For example, the 6 of Pentacles is attributed to the moon in Taurus. It's the second of three cards (in the Minor Arcana) associated with Taurus. This correlates with the second ten-day period of that sign, the beginning of May. For a complete list of astrological attributions for both Majors and Minors, see **Tip #43: Astrology in a Tarot Reading**.

Tip #43: Astrology in a Tarot Reading

QUESTION:

I've been learning how to read the cards for about six months now, I got interested after a reading in a store. I have one question about the way my cards were read. Before the reading started, my reader asked me what star sign I was. I know that this helps with the reading, but the spread seemed to start off from a specific card according to my answer. Do you know what this spread is? It looked like a variation of the Celtic Cross, but I can't be sure. I have looked in plenty of books, but haven't found any clues. — Jay

ANSWER:

This particular method does not sound familiar to me, but many readers create their own spreads and it could be that this was the case with your reading. However, since you believe that the spread was a variation on the Celtic Cross, there's another possibility.

Since the Celtic Cross does not have astrological attributions assigned to the positions in the spread, my guess is that the reader used his or her knowledge of the astrological associations of the cards themselves to find a starting point. For your reference, here is a list of sun signs and the cards related to them according to a standard and widely used system of attributions that we follow at The Tarot School. (You may find other systems of attribution elsewhere.)

Aries = The Emperor

Taurus = The Hierophant

Gemini = The Lovers

Cancer = The Chariot

Leo = Strength

Virgo = The Hermit

Libra = Justice

Scorpio = Death

Sagittarius = Temperance

Capricorn = The Devil

Aquarius = The Star

Pisces = The Moon

If the reading began with a Minor Arcana card, most likely the Element associated with the season of your birth was the determining factor:

Suit of Swords = Air Signs: Gemini, Libra, Aquarius

Suit of Wands = Fire Signs: Aries, Leo, Sagittarius

Suit of Cups = Water Signs: Cancer, Scorpio, Pisces

Suit of Pentacles = Earth Signs: Taurus, Virgo, Capricorn

More complex astrological associations can be made as well, but chances are they were not considered in this context. One other possibility is that the reader did a numerological reduction of your birth date and began with that position. This technique of the querent's birth energy in a reading can be applied to any spread.

If you have a good working knowledge of astrology, you may find these more specific associations for the Minor Arcana interesting. As always, there are other systems of attribution, but this is the one we prefer:

Suit of Swords (Element of Air):   Ace = the season of Spring

Cardinal Air	*Fixed Air*	*Mutable Air*
2 = Moon in Libra	5 = Venus in Aquarius	8 = Jupiter in Gemini
3 = Saturn in Libra	6 = Mercury in Aquarius	9 = Mars in Gemini
4 = Jupiter in Libra	7 = Moon in Aquarius	10 = Sun in Gemini

Suit of Wands (Element of Fire):   Ace = the season of Summer

Cardinal Fire	*Fixed Fire*	*Mutable Fire*
2 = Mars in Aries	5 = Saturn in Leo	8 = Mercury in Sagittarius
3 = Sun in Aries	6 = Jupiter in Leo	9 = Moon in Sagittarius
4 = Venus in Aries	7 = Mars in Leo	10 = Saturn in Sagittarius

Suit of Cups (Element of Water):   Ace = the season of Autumn

Cardinal Water	*Fixed Water*	*Mutable Water*
2 = Venus in Cancer	5 = Mars in Scorpio	8 = Saturn in Pisces
3 = Mercury in Cancer	6 = Sun in Scorpio	9 = Jupiter in Pisces
4 = Moon in Cancer	7 = Venus in Scorpio	10 = Mars in Pisces

Suit of Pentacles (Element of Earth):   Ace = the season of Winter

Cardinal Earth	*Fixed Earth*	*Mutable Earth*
2 = Jupiter in Capricorn	5 = Mercury in Taurus	8 = Sun in Virgo
3 = Mars in Capricorn	6 = Moon in Taurus	9 = Venus in Virgo
4 = Sun in Capricorn	7 = Saturn in Taurus	10 = Mercury in Virgo

If you assign the four Aces to the seasons, thirty-six cards remain in the numbered cards of the Minor Arcana, nine per suit. Each of these coincides with ten degrees of the circle of the year, and each of these ten degree sections is called a "decan." Since a sign contains 30 degrees, there are three decans to each sign. For example: the 2 of Wands is attributed to the first decan of the sign of Leo and runs from 0–10 degrees. The second decan (3 of Wands) runs from 11–20 degrees of Leo. And the third decan (4 of Wands) runs from 21–30 degrees of Leo. This pattern is repeated throughout all the signs.

Tip #44: Using Esotericism in a Reading

Ever wonder what to do with all those tables of correspondences you come across in books? Here's a simple reading exercise we teach in class that can help you use some of that information in a practical way.

1. Divide your deck into two stacks—one comprised of the Major Arcana cards, and the other of the remaining cards.

2. Formulate your question.

3. Shuffle each stack while concentrating on your question and place the cards face-down in front of you.

4. Draw two cards from the Minor Arcana pile, using any method you like. These two cards will give you a basic answer to your question. It is not necessary for them to have any particular position assignments but feel free to assign some if that makes you more comfortable.

5. Draw one card from the Major Arcana pile. Do *not* interpret this card in the usual manner. Instead, choose an esoteric correspondence associated with the card to give you additional information. The only purpose of this card is to point the way toward this hidden bit of information.

We did several readings using this technique that were remarkably insightful. There are many sources of correspondences, but the ones that we worked with in class were the Golden Dawn astrological attributions and esoteric functions:

Card	Astro. Attribution	Esoteric Function
The Fool	Air	(No function)
The Magician	Mercury	Life & Death
The High Priestess	Moon	Peace & War
The Empress	Venus	Wisdom & Folly
The Emperor	Aries	Sight
The Hierophant	Taurus	Hearing
The Lovers	Gemini	Smell
The Chariot	Cancer	Speech
Strength	Leo	Taste
The Hermit	Virgo	Sexuality (Touch)
Wheel of Fortune	Jupiter	Riches & Poverty
Justice	Libra	Work
The Hanged Man	Water	(No function)
Death	Scorpio	Movement
Temperance	Sagittarius	Anger
The Devil	Capricorn	Laughter
The Tower	Mars	Indignation & Grace
The Star	Aquarius	Imagination
The Moon	Pisces	Sleep
The Sun	Sun	Fertility & Barrenness
Judgement	Fire	(No function)
The World	Saturn	Power & Servitude

In doing this reading, it's wise to use reversals. For example, in the case of those cards that have double functions, an upright card would indicate the first of the functions mentioned and a reversal would indicate the second function.

Even the cards that have only one function have two clearly different versions of that function. For example, the Emperor has the function of sight. Reversed, it could mean blindness or the inability to "see." Justice has the function of work. Reversed, it could mean not working or something that has malfunctioned.

You can use the astrological attributions to give you insight into the types of energy that are influencing the situation, to represent people with that particular sun sign, or to help with questions of timing.

If you choose to work with more extensive tables of correspondence, remember to keep it simple—pick one (or two at the most) to help you zero in on the hidden answer to your question.

Tip #45: Complex Reading Technique

Sometimes you can combine a whole series of one-, two-, and three-card readings into a comprehensive series that answers every question a querent may have on a complex topic. In this way, it's possible for them to ask one question after another concerning a particular subject and get a straightforward, powerful answer to each facet of their main concern.

Everyone knows, for example, most readings are about romance and relationships. Romantic issues often have many twists and turns, and a single answer to a general question is not altogether satisfying. The querent may have many things they'd like to know about their present situation.

The way this technique works is to help the querent formulate a specific question and answer it with a one-, two-, or three-card spread. Then use the answer as a springboard for further questions, each answered with its own one-, two-, or three-card spread.

To begin the technique, shuffle and cut in the usual way. Do one short spread and leave it face-up on the table. Without reshuffling, answer the next question with another short spread, drawing the cards off the top of the deck. Set this second spread face-up, directly beneath the first one. Then do a third, a fourth, etc. Do as many such short spreads as are necessary to cover every aspect of the querent's issue.

In this way, you organically create a large, subtle, complex spread that is made of easily managed parts. The entire history of the question, and all its answers, are laid out on the table for you and the querent to see clearly.

Tip #46: Bottoms Up!

Let's get to the bottom of this!

Want to find out the underlying influence in a situation? Or maybe a subconscious motive or desire? Look at the card on the bottom of the deck. It never fails to give some additional insight.

Tip #47: Reversed Readings

QUESTION:

I have been having a dickens of a time. I did a reading for my husband and all the cards came out upright and beautiful. However, when I try to do a reading for myself lately, every single card has come up reversed. I simply shake my head, clear the deck, and walk away. Do you have any ideas what may be doing this? It has been happening now for about two weeks. Before that I would get an occasional reversed card. — Marsha

ANSWER:

If a spread contains only reversed cards, Wald and I tend to ignore the reversals and read the spread as if they were all upright. In a case like this, we take the reversals to be the cards' way of drawing extra attention to themselves. (This is one of many ways we look at reversals, and you can certainly use this interpretation for single reversed cards as well.)

In your case, Marsha, it would seem that rather than shaking your head and walking away, you might want to turn the cards upright and take the time to give them some serious thought. My sense is that the deck is trying very hard to get your attention—even going so far as to stand on its head! Once you have gotten the message, my bet is this unusual occurrence will stop and your readings will return to more familiar patterns.

Tip #48: Many Majors in a Spread

QUESTION:

Lately, every time I do a weekly reading for myself, I get five or six Majors. The recurring ones are: the High Priestess, the Fool, the Hanged Man, the Chariot, and the Hermit.

This confuses me. I turn to the Tarot for its wisdom, and hopefully find my way. Years back, The Tower kept showing up, and yes, I experienced the crisis of The Tower. I know that is behind me now. I live a more reflective life compared to few years back.

Also, how often can one read for oneself? — Bonnie

ANSWER:

Oftentimes, the questions we ask are only the surface aspect of deeper questions of which we're not conscious. Even purely practical questions sometimes serve as disguises for deeper issues. Then, practical matters become like the elements of dreams—turning us back on ourselves for reflection and contemplation.

When a disproportionate number of Majors turn up in a spread, the first thing to consider is the need to look deeper than the initial question. When this happens repeatedly, it's almost a guarantee that the cards are asking you for greater subtlety and self-inquiry.

In order to reach deeper levels of meaning, it's really good to know as many levels of interpretations of each card as possible, including:

- Practical
- Psychological
- Esoteric
- Spiritual

For example, let's look at one of your recurring cards, the Hermit.

On a practical level, the Hermit speaks of the need for solitude, of being clear and pure in intention and action, of striving for the highest and of being a model and guide to others.

Psychologically, the Hermit addresses the issues of detachment, personal attainment, self-improvement, and total commitment to a high goal (never looking backward or downward).

Some of the esoteric considerations of this card include the astrological attribution of Virgo (and all that implies), combined with the sexual fire contained in the connection with the Hebrew letter Yod. This can produce either a powerful restrained or repressed sexual impulse, or a sublimated sexual energy that often expresses itself as spiritual ambition.

On a spiritual level, the Hermit distills light from his own purity. And where that light shines, it dispels the darkness of the personal shadow. When the Hermit is active on this level, you can expect a powerful realization and a new level of understanding to reveal itself.

There is considerably more to each level than there is room to mention here, but you get the idea. The Majors can work on any one of these levels or on several at the same time. You'll instinctively know which ones apply to your present situation. The more you know about each card, the deeper you can go.

In answer to your question about how often you can read for yourself, our experience shows that you can read as often as you like. Instead of thinking of each reading as separate, you can regard successive readings as a continuous process—each reading deepening the ones before it. Sometimes though, the deck will actually get annoyed with you for pestering it and it will let you know when enough is enough.

Tip #49: Contradictory Cards

QUESTION:

My question has to do with interpreting seemingly very opposing cards in a spread. I recently did a reading for myself about a painful relationship that I've decided to back off from. I did a reading to get some insight on the situation and these are the confusing cards that came up:

In the "covers you" position was the 3 of Cups, right next to it in the "crosses you" position was the 3 of Swords, while the card representing "other" was the Sun.

Another reading showed the 10 of Cups in the "significator" position, 2 of Cups in the "near future" position, but the "outcome" card was the Lovers card reversed.

Can you speak, in a general sense, about how one should begin to interpret seemingly highly contradictory cards in a reading? What role does their position in the spread play? — Susan

ANSWER:

I'm not sure of the best way to answer your question, Susan, because as far as we're concerned, cards never really contradict themselves. The trick is to understand the full range of meanings for each card in order to see where it fits in the scheme of things. Another important thing to keep in mind is that although two cards may *look* as though they're talking about the same thing, they may not be.

For instance, in the second example you gave, the 2 of Cups appeared in the "near future" position while the Lovers turned up reversed in the "outcome." Do these cards really contradict themselves or are they just different aspects of the story?

The first thing to remember is that if you are working with a spread that has fixed positions, those positions will play a strong part in suggesting the appropriate interpretation for the card. The "near future" and the "outcome" are not the same thing. If they were, we wouldn't need two different positions.

So the 2 of Cups could indicate a coming together while the Lovers reversed might be saying either (1) it won't work out in the long run or (2) because this new relationship (2 of Cups) is so hot, you're going to dump the old one (Lovers reversed)! Those two cards may not be talking about the same things at all.

Some cards in a reading will be talking about the querent's state of mind while others will address what's actually happening. Again, these are not necessarily compatible energies and can look like contradictions on the surface. The 3 of Swords accurately describes the challenge you face in backing off from your painful relationship. However, the 3 of Cups may be where your head is—a positive and cheerful attitude that will help you bounce back quickly and which is reinforced by the presence of the Sun.

If you do any spread with more than one card, the cards you pull will interact with each other even if there are no set positions. Let's take a random example of two cards where it might be difficult to see the connection at first glance—the 10 of Swords and the 4 of Wands.

Depending upon the question (which is always the most important thing to keep in mind when choosing the appropriate interpretations), you might have:

- Someone dying at home.

- Domestic abuse.

- The end of one phase of life and the beginning of another.

- Recovery after a serious illness.

- Making lemonade out of lemons.

- A change of residence.

- Reaching the limit of people you can invite to a wedding or other affair.

I'm sure if you think about it, you could come up with many more possible interpretations for this combination.

The main things to keep in mind when integrating any cards in a reading are:

- What is the question?

- What's going on in the querent's environment?

- How does the querent's mental state affect things?

- How many different ways can you interpret each card?

- Which one(s) make the most sense? (Sometimes, you can read a single card on two or more levels.)

- If a card doesn't seem to make any sense, consider it may be addressing a related but different matter.

If you're really stumped, sleep on it. Give the reading some time to percolate in your subconscious and you may see things you missed the first time.

One more option you may have is to ask another reader for their perspective. Sometimes their opinion can give you another way of looking at the reading that will help clarify things for you.

Tip #50: Repeated Readings

QUESTION:

I have had people hate a reading and demand another one. Is it ever acceptable to redo the reading? Some say only one reading in twenty-four hours, and one article I read said one a week.

I was also taught that the reading was for that moment in time and one cannot do another reading as this will negate the message of the first one. I would appreciate your experiences with this. — Barb

ANSWER:

Have you ever sat around at night and talked with a friend about some weighty matter and discussed it until you got tired and both of you knew you'd talked enough?

Doing multiple readings in a short time about the same issue is like that. There's no harm in it. Each successive reading simply deepens or adds to the previous ones, rather than negating them. You can view continuous readings as a continuous discussion— and as with a discussion, you can continue until you're tired. No harm.

When your "discussion" stops making sense, it's time to stop. The cards will let you know.

Tip #51: Cold Reading

Did you know that there's a simple Tarot reading technique that you can use to give a person a reading without using the cards?

It's called a cold reading and uses a technique which we call *The Voice in the Card*. To use this technique in a reading, draw a card and then let your eyes wander over the images in the card.

Eventually, your attention will be caught by a small detail in the picture. That detail will have a message for the querent—a message that will most likely have nothing to do with the traditional interpretation of the card.

For example, in the *RWS* 9 of Pentacles, there is a little snail in the bottom left portion of the picture. If this was the detail that caught your eye, the message might involve slowing down, having patience, or protection of some kind. Or perhaps, you might suggest that the querent have dinner at a fancy French restaurant.

In a cold reading, the *querent* is the card. Take a good look at the person you're reading for. Notice their clothing, jewelry, posture. Notice their hair, facial expression, etc. Find the detail that holds your attention more than any other.

This detail will tell you something important about this person. It will give you information that you wouldn't know just by looking at them. This is different than just being aware of body language—it goes deeper than that.

There are three guidelines to follow when giving your message:

1. Let the message be true.

2. Let it be useful.

3. If possible, let the message be surprising.

You can use this technique in conjunction with reading the cards or you can use it with anyone at any time under any circumstances. The more you practice, the better you get. Have fun!

QUESTION:

I love the idea of cold readings. I can see how this could be a great help in everyday life situations—to help yourself, to help others. What about when you get up in the morning and choose to wear something and look at yourself in the mirror to check yourself out before leaving the house, or just staying home—couldn't you do a cold reading for yourself, too, in order to prepare for the day?
— Dorothy

ANSWER:

That's a great idea, Dorothy. Why not give it a try? You may find that it's harder to do this for yourself at first, but with practice, it sounds like it could be very useful.

Tip #52: Reading for Yourself

QUESTION:

I have a question about reading cards for myself. Specifically, I read much better for strangers and friends, but certainly best for the former. As for reading for myself, I read too much into it! Do you have an insight about how to clear my mind when the subject matter is up close and personal? — Jacqueline

ANSWER:

The perceived difficulty of reading for ourselves comes from our assumption that we need to be objective at all times, and that only objectivity is valuable. Since we are more intimate with friends than we are with strangers, and more intimate with ourselves than we are with friends, objectivity really isn't possible.

When reading for yourself, you have to make use of *subjectivity* instead. In *all* readings, you want to bring to bear everything you know—your life experience, your knowledge of the cards, your empathy with your subject, your intuition—everything! You can do all of this with yourself.

Make use of the intimacy you have with yourself—don't be afraid of it, or feel that it is somehow wrong because you are too close. If you get multiple impressions and/or messages, that's okay. Make a note of all of them. Sit with them for awhile. Eventually, the important messages will stick with you and everything else will fade.

When you're reading for yourself, you have a lot more time to think and reflect about what the cards have told you than you would if you were reading for a stranger. Take advantage of that.

Reading for yourself is a technique—like all techniques, it takes time to learn and you will get better with practice.

Tip #53: Tarot and Discipline

QUESTION:

I am not new to Tarot, nor am I very disciplined about my study and practice. Recently I took Joan Bunning's online Tarot course at Barnes & Noble University and found it to be very helpful. Now that the classes are over, though, I haven't managed to discipline myself to do the daily card reading. It is not from lack of interest. I wonder if you have run into this before, and if you have any tips that might help. — Isha

ANSWER:

Have I encountered trouble with discipline? All the time! I'm more disciplined about some things than others, and that's no doubt true for you as well. The subject of discipline itself is large enough to fill books, but let's focus on how it relates to your study and practice of Tarot.

Here are a couple of things you might consider:

1. **Redefine Discipline**
   Most of us have been brought up to equate discipline with a particular behavior, often requiring effort that is repeated or maintained over a long period of time. While this is a valid definition of the word, we sometimes interpret the definition a little too narrowly and impose limits upon ourselves unnecessarily. There is no rule that says you have to pull a card every day. Unless

this particular practice really lights your fire, you could begin to see the daily draw as a chore—and we often have a natural resistance to chores.

Introducing flexibility into your practices can be much more productive in the long run. If you want a steady routine but find the daily schedule too much, try choosing a card every other day, or once a week, instead.

You mentioned that you are not new to Tarot. Shift your perspective a little and use the word "discipline" to encompass all the ways you have incorporated Tarot into your life over the years. From that point of view you could say that your personal Tarot discipline encompasses any number of things including reading books, taking classes, reading for friends and/or clients, meditation, experimentation, discussing Tarot with colleagues, keeping a Tarot journal, asking questions (such as this one), and reading for yourself—whether it's a card-a-day or complex spreads. One day you'll do one thing, the next something else. You might skip a week, or a month or more, and then pick up on it again. As long as you maintain your interest and activity over a long period of time, you have discipline. Surprise!

2. Play With Others

Not everybody is well suited to working on their own, however, and you may find yourself in this category. In that case, the best thing to do is to join a class, such as you just did. The group energy of the students, combined with direction from a good teacher, provides the kind of momentum that is very hard to generate on one's own. There are several sources of interactive instruction:

• **Local**
Check your local metaphysical shop to see if they have any classes or know of anyone offering Tarot instruction in your area. You may also find a continuing education class at a nearby high school or college. Also check with

any mainstream bookstores to see if they host a monthly class. Another method of finding a local class is to use the search engines. Enter "Tarot" and (put the name of your town or state here), i.e., "Tarot and Amherst" or "Tarot and Connecticut" (without the quotes). Of course, if you live in the New York City area, don't forget us at The Tarot School. We hold live classes every week.

- **Online**
  The Internet is a great source of online courses and discussion lists. Some lists actually give assignments which are then shared among the group. Search under "Tarot" at YahooGroups, Topica, and the like.

- **Professional Association**
  Join the American Tarot Association and take advantage of their wonderful mentor program. You can have a mentor help you with your own studies and you can also become a mentor for others. It's true what they say about learning much more once you begin to teach! Visit their website at: **http://www.ata-tarot.com**

- **Telephone**
  The Tarot School offers classes on the telephone. These are totally interactive and have the added advantage that you can participate in the class wherever you have access to a phone. For The Tarot School's current schedule of telecourses, visit:
  http://www.TarotSchool.com/Seminars.html

- **Correspondence Courses**
  Tarot correspondence courses are available from a number of reputable teachers and organizations. (Your favorite search engine will help you find them.) All of them will add structure to your study but they have varying levels of interactivity. *The Tarot School Correspondence Course* can be taken as a self-study course or as a degree program for serious students that includes

in-depth personal coaching sessions.
http://www.TarotSchool.com/Course.html

You'll probably find that a comfortable mix of private practice and group participation will go the farthest in sustaining your interest and enthusiasm for Tarot. Tarot is a growing and dynamic field and there are so many ways it can nurture our spirit and delight our intellect. Whatever form your discipline takes, enjoy it immensely!

FOUR

SPREADS

The practical language of Tarot is a language of question and answer. In that language, card meanings could be compared to the words, and spreads to the grammar. Spreads are the way a reader presents questions to the oracle of Tarot and receives answers in return.

This grammar of question and answer has been evolving as long as Tarot has itself, and it has become so elaborate that it can answer just about any question you could think to ask, but to be useful, a spread must be read. The answer it contains has to be interpreted, then communicated to the querent, the questioner. This is the skill of distilling meaning from a spread and saying what you see in a clear and appropriate manner. It is a skill that can be refined to a very high level, and there is virtually no limit to the amount of time you can usefully spend in learning to do it better and better.

The drama of human life has an almost infinite variety of nuance and detail, but there is a remarkably small number of basic issues that concern us all. It is for this reason that Tarot readings use spreads.

Essentially, every spread is a template, specially designed to address a particular issue and answer a range of questions arising from it. If there were an infinity of issues, there would have to be an infinity of spreads to deal with them. Luckily, that is not the case, but there is still a dazzling array to choose from.

In every book or collection of spreads, a representative sampling is offered from among hundreds of possibilities that seems to cover the issues that concern us most—love, money, health, and career, for example. This chapter is no exception, and although for reasons of space our selection is limited, the spreads you will find here are unusual and highly effective. You will also find a useful list of good books and websites that make an excellent resource for spreads of all types.

Tip #54: A Powerful One-Card Reading

I'm going to share this tip in the form of a personal story. I had the pleasure of getting a quick one-card reading from one of our students in the Monday night class. I was called for jury duty that week and had served my first day as part of a large group of people who were being considered for the jury in a homicide case. This particular trial was expected to last about a month. I asked the question: "How long will I be on jury duty?"

The card I chose was the 10 of Pentacles (*Universal Waite*). When I saw it, my first instinct was "Oh great, I'm going to be there for ten weeks—or at the very least, ten days." But since I wasn't the one doing the reading, I waited patiently to hear the student's interpretation. He used a technique that we teach called *The Voice in the Card*. In this reading, standard or traditional meanings of the cards are completely disregarded. It is a purely intuitive reading derived only from the visual imagery in the card.

The reader let his eyes wander over all the pictorial elements in the card until his attention was held by one particular detail that contained the message for me. He took his time. Finally, he pointed to the image of the two greyhounds near the bottom of the scene and told me that I would only have to serve for two days.

I told him that while a two-day stint was my personal wish, I couldn't possibly imagine how that could be. At the very least, I thought, I would be there until the end of the week. Even so, he stuck by his interpretation. To make a long story short, the next day it was my turn to be questioned by the judge and the lawyers. I was not selected, was sent back to central jury and shortly thereafter was dismissed and sent home. Two dogs—two days.

In this example, the question was one of timing. However, this is one of the best ways we know of to answer absolutely any question at all. *The Voice in the Card* can be used as the basis for a powerful one-card reading or it can be integrated into any other spread you choose.

QUESTION:

My question is how do I obtain the card for a one-card reading? Does the querent draw it? Do I shuffle and draw it? Is it a random card in the already thrown spread? — Angela

ANSWER:

Any or all of the above methods will work equally well. You can use this technique as a one-card reading or you can choose a card from any multicard spread and use it there. It's *especially* handy if you're drawing a blank on a particular card, because you don't need to know anything about the card's traditional meaning in order to intuit the card's message.

Tip #55: Yes/No Spread

Every now and then someone will ask if we know a good Yes/No spread that is consistent and reliable. This question itself could serve as an example of the difficulty of giving an unambiguous answer to a simple question. We would have to answer this question, "Well, sort of."

When occasion demands, we use several variations of a Yes/No technique we learned from Gina Pace. Our results with it vary as much as they do with any spread. Is it accurate and dependable? Probably. Are our interpretation and the answers we give equally reliable? No. We are, after all, fallible.

That said, there are many people who just aren't comfortable without a Yes/No spread as part of their repertoire, so here's the one we use:

Variation #1

After the question has been asked, and refined to the greatest possible level of clarity, have the querent draw a single card. Ask the querent to tell you how the card makes them feel when they first see it. Instinctively. Intuitively. Does the card make their spirits rise, or does it make their stomach sink when they look at it?

This is the key. A good feeling about the card, based entirely on an immediate, intuitive response to the picture, equals the answer the querent wants to hear. A negative feeling indicates the opposite. The stronger the feeling, the more unambiguous the answer.

But that leads to another issue. Does the querent prefer a Yes or No answer? You'll need to clarify that before doing the reading.

It has been our experience that this method works quite well in the majority of cases.

Variation #2

Draw three cards and lay them out in a row. Let the middle card serve the same function as the single card in Variation #1. Let the two flanking cards serve as commentary, and a source of additional information.

Variation #3

Draw five cards. Read these in the same way as in Variation #2, with the added information and commentary of two additional cards. Our own tendency is to give the supporting cards greater weight as they approach the center.

Variation #4

In a three- or five-card spread, simply count the number of upright and reversed cards. A majority of upright cards gives a "Yes" answer. A majority of reversed cards gives a "No" answer. Give the center card more weight and importance than the others.

The more completely this spread has a particular orientation, the more unequivocal the answer. For example, in a five-card spread:

All 5 cards Upright:	A resounding Yes!
3 or 4 Upright (including Center):	A very likely Yes
3 or 4 Upright (not including Center):	A probable Yes
3 or 4 Reversed (not including Center):	A probable No
3 or 4 Reversed (including Center):	A very likely No
All 5 cards Reversed:	A resounding No!

Don't forget to use the meanings of the cards to add specifics and depth to your answer.

Here's the real tip, though. Do your best to rephrase your question so that it is not answered by a simple Yes or No. For instance, instead of asking, "Will I get this job?" try something like "How favorable are my chances of getting this job?" Create a spread that will include cards that look at your interview, the chemistry with your potential employer, your talent for the job, your competition, salary, etc. A reading like this can be informative and illuminating. Much more useful than Yes or No.

Tip #56: Reading Spreads Without Assigned Positions

QUESTION:

I have been told by some people that they do not use spreads for all readings. I wonder if you could discuss this. I am not so much interested in pros and cons of using spreads or not using them, but more interested in finding out what the people who don't use spreads with assigned positions are actually doing. I do readings on a free site, and they gave us a file of spreads and said they would prefer that we use spreads. I have only ever used spreads, even if they were just custom-made spreads. I am just very unclear about what people are doing alternative to the kind of spreads I'm familiar with. — Marcia

ANSWER:

I often read using spreads without assigned positions. There's really nothing too mysterious about reading that way if you understand the basic principle that any card can answer any question. You can use the *Voice in the Card* technique at any time (see **Tip #55: A Powerful One-Card Spread**), whether you're reading with one card or many.

Another technique is to develop a continuous story. Start your reading with one card and then choose additional cards to give you more information or tell you what will likely happen next.

A favorite reading style we use in class is to lay out three cards in a horizontal row. Read them as multiple facets of a single jewel, each card giving a little more information or insight. Interpret the card in the center first as it will contain the answer to the question. The cards on either side will offer commentary and can be read in any order you choose. Look for any patterns among the three cards, such as repeated numbers or suits, to add an additional layer of interpretation to your reading.

Some people just start throwing cards on the table at a great rate, without any apparent spread positions. Competent readers who do this pick out the relevant information from a rapid flow of cards in a form of free association that can produce remarkable results. Sometimes this technique is used by psychics as a buffer to make their clients feel more comfortable. And, of course, there are those who use this method to disguise their lack of knowledge of the cards.

Personally, I believe that if you focus your attention on one card at a time, as if it were the only card you had to answer the question, you'll wind up using fewer cards, doing deeper readings, and concerning yourself less with assigning positions. There are times when it's more appropriate to work with positions and other times when they're unnecessary. I don't advocate one method over the other—it's all good!

Tip #57: The Double-Edged Sword Spread

QUESTION:

The other day I got a check in the mail for freelance work I had forgotten about and so it was like free money (so to speak). Anyway, I had been planning to buy myself either a new Zip drive or a new 35mm automated camera and could not (and still cannot) decide which to use this money for. So I was going to consult the cards but realized I had no idea what kind of a spread I should use. I know how to get a Yes/No answer and some of the more standard spreads but none of those seemed to be appropriate for this situation. Any suggestions? — JP

ANSWER:

The best spread to use in a case like this is one we call *The Double-Edged Sword*. We gave it this name because it is in the shape of a sword (long and double-edged) and because it utilizes the *energy* of the suit of Swords to help bring clarity and discrimination to difficult decisions. This spread is useful any time a choice must be made between one of two real options. Examples in addition to the question asked above include choices between relationships, job offers, moving locations, career paths, etc.

The layout is very simple. After shuffling the cards, cut the entire deck into two piles. Assign one pile for Choice #1 and the other pile for Choice #2. From the first pile, draw five cards and place them in a vertical line on the table. Draw five more cards from the second pile and place them in a second vertical line, next to the first.

Although the layout is simple, the interpretation is very subtle. There are no specific positions assigned to these cards. Each row is read as a multifaceted picture of the energies and likely outcome of that particular path. A chronology of events may suggest itself but try not to approach the reading as a series of chronological steps—look at each group of five cards as a whole.

Sometimes the answer will be obvious. More often though, both options will have their pros and cons. The cards will verify things you already know and point out things you may not have considered. Compare the two sides and notice the strengths and trouble spots in each. In addition to any objective information you receive, the images in the cards have the power to evoke emotional responses. Consider these responses, as well, when making your decision.

This spread can be expanded to consider a third option by starting with three piles and laying out three vertical rows, but any more than that would diminish the clarity of the reading.

Tip #58: Relationship Spreads

QUESTION:

Could you tell me how to read a spread involving the relationship between two people? How do you interpret what goes with which person?

ANSWER:

Designate specific positions for both yourself and your partner before you begin the reading. One technique is to have separate rows or columns for each person. By creating the spread yourself, you have the best chance at getting the information you really need.

Another approach is to focus on the issues that are important to you as a couple. This is a very personal process so take some time and think about this. Here are some suggestions to get you started:

1. What is the basis of our attraction?

2. How sexually compatible are we?

3. How emotionally available is this person?

4. Can we be supportive of each other?

5. Can we laugh and have fun together?

6. Are our spiritual paths compatible?

7. How well will we deal with money?

8. How balanced will our relationship be?

9. Is my partner ready for and/or capable of commitment?

10. Am I ready for and/or capable of commitment?

11. How will our families interact?

12. What kind of parent will my partner be?

This is just an example of the types of issues one might want some insight into. That said, I personally feel the most important thing to do when dealing with relationship issues is to pay attention to your partner and to your heart. The cards can give you perspective but don't let them take the fun out of exploring and discovering your partner for yourself. Of course, since at least 95 percent of the questions you'll ever get from clients are about relationships, you probably wouldn't stay in business long if you told them that.

Tip #59: New Year's Spread

Many people enjoy the tradition of doing an annual New Year's reading. Simply draw one card for each month of the year and place them in a circular pattern with January at the top. Take a moment to write the cards down. You'll want to keep this record in your notebook or someplace safe to refer to throughout the year.

Instead of interpreting the cards one month at a time, look at each group of three cards as describing the energy for each season. All three cards will be active simultaneously during those three months.

See how any other spreads you throw during the course of the coming year relate to the three cards of the appropriate season.

Tip #60: Year-Long Spread

The Year-Long Spread is not really a tip, but a Tarot practice. In order to do this spread properly, you will need to know your birth cards. Please see **Tip #69: Determining Your Birth Cards**, for the method we use—it is different from others you may have come across.

This is another spread that is good to begin at the New Year, but you may start it any time. It is a combination of a spread and a practice that is done every day for a year. At the end of that time you may, if you wish, continue your practice with a new spread.

A day is a long time. A year has 365 of them—almost an eternity. As mentioned previously, it's a common practice among Tarotists to pick a card every day and contemplate its message. This spread will elaborate on that practice and give you a mighty piece of contemplation to do.

For this exercise you will need a dedicated deck that you won't use for anything else during the coming year. Prepare a special place to keep and refer to the cards you will be using for this exercise. There will never be more than five of them at a time so you won't need a big space. Your desk or altar might do very nicely.

First, take your two birth cards out of the deck.

Second, make a separate deck out of the Major Arcana (minus your birth cards) and draw one card from this little deck for the year. Contemplate this card as your theme for the year. Spend some time every day for the next year doing at least a small contemplation on this card. Contemplate this year card in the context of your birth cards.

Third, shuffle the remaining Major Arcana back into the rest of the deck. Now pick one from this deck as your theme for the month. Contemplate this card within the context of the year card and your birth cards. These cards together will contain an augmented message for the month.

Each month, return the previous month's card to the deck and draw a new card for the new month. Fourth, shuffle the remaining cards of the deck carefully and thoroughly once each day and then draw a card for the day. Add this card to the other four and contemplate the five cards together as your message for the day.

If you do this Five-Card Contemplation each day, changing the day and the month cards at the appropriate times, by the end of the year, your sense of yourself, your year, and Tarot will be very intricate, very detailed, very large, and very true. Our students who have worked with this technique have found it to be powerful practice.

The following questions and answers should clear up any confusion you might have about the process:

QUESTION:

I have some questions regarding the Year-Long Spread:

1. What do you do when the person has just one birth card? Would you just have four cards in the spread? An example would be my husband with the birthdate: $1 + 19 + 19 + 31 = 70 = 7$.

2. What do you mean when you say this implies a higher octave?

3. Any particular tips for contemplating the cards?

I am glad to know about this spread and plan to use it for this year. I suspect doing this will be very fruitful! Thank you very much. — Georgia

ANSWER:

Thanks, Georgia—we're happy you like the spread! Questions 1 and 2 can be answered together. Except for the 19/10/1 combination (see below), birth cards always come in pairs. The "higher octave" just refers to the card that has the higher number.

If your birthdate number adds up to a two-digit number ending in zero (i.e., 50, 60, 70, etc.), it reduces directly to a single-digit number. But each single-digit number in Tarot is a reduction of one of the double-digit numbers.

So in your husband's case, for example, 70 reduces to 7, but 7 is a direct reduction of 16.

For easy reference, here's a list of the pairs:

21–The World / 3–The Empress

20–Judgement / 2–The High Priestess

19–The Sun / 10–The Wheel of Fortune / 1–The Magician

18–The Moon / 9–The Hermit

17–The Star / 8–Strength

16–The Tower / 7–The Chariot

15–The Devil / 6–The Lovers

14–Temperance / 5–The Hierophant

13–Death / 4–The Emperor

12–The Hanged Man / 3–The Empress

11–Justice / 2–The High Priestess

10–The Wheel of Fortune / 1–The Magician

You'll notice that both the High Priestess and the Empress can be paired with two different cards. For example, 20 reduces to 2 and 11 also reduces to 2. Twenty doesn't reduce to 11, so this is not a triple birth card combination—you'll have either one pair or the other.

As for your third question, we're glad you asked! Contemplation is easier to do than to explain. It's mostly holding an idea or an image in your attention without thinking about it too hard. A lot of times, your conscious mind gets in the way of the deep stuff that comes from lower down in your understanding. If you don't analyze or impose prelearned formulas and definitions on the object of your contemplation, your intuition and some unknown wisdom inside you will suggest things that are quite amazing— that you could never have thought of intentionally.

I guess the idea is to mentally relax while holding an image or a thought in your mind. Then, the mind will "melt" the thought the way your mouth melts a hard candy without chewing on it. Then the sweet center will eventually be released.

Contemplations can be short or long, a couple of minutes, or extended over a few days. The best times for contemplation are just after waking up and just before going to sleep. At those times, your logical controls have begun to soften and you have greater access to the creative layer that is usually suppressed. Also, if you can, write down what comes up in your contemplations. If you don't, they'll evaporate like dreams.

QUESTION:

In the section regarding birth cards, the numerology of 11 = 2 is discussed, but what about 22 = 4? Should 22 be considered the Fool? Or should only the 4 be used? I would think that the Fool would qualify as card #22, as it is the 22nd Major Arcana card, but it is given the value of 0 in the deck, so I am not sure how to treat this. Also, since it is a "master number," as are 11 and 33, is there any other significance that should be considered?

ANSWER:

The Fool is numbered 0 in some decks and is unnumbered in other decks. No combination of numbers reduces to 0—therefore, in our system, we do not consider it as a possible birth card. "Master" numbers are specific to numerology, which is a different system altogether and so also do not apply.

This is not to negate the value of master numbers or to dismiss the Fool as an unimportant card. We just don't use them in this particular work.

QUESTION:

I'm having a little trouble determining a birth card that adds up to 100. If the date is as follows: 08 + 20 + 19 + 53 = 100, how do I figure out the birth card?

ANSWER:

With a sum of 100 (or any three-digit number), treat the first two digits as a single number and add it to the third. In your case, just add 10 + 0. The answer is 10, the Wheel of Fortune, which reduces to 1 (1 + 0 = 1), the Magician.

Tip #61: Yule Reading

QUESTION:

Just wanted to ask if there were any readings or meditations y'all knew of for the Yule season? — JP

ANSWER:

I have to admit, there isn't any particular technique that I've consistently used but one of my favorite things is to make up techniques to fit the occasion—literally in this case.

Rather than give you a particular layout or meditation, however, I'm going to suggest some guidelines that will help you design your own. This can be a very powerful practice.

The most important part of this process is to get in touch with the symbolism of this season and how it relates to your own life. Yule specifically celebrates the rebirth of the sun at the darkest time of year. This can be viewed as the return of hope, light, and growth after a period of darkness and contraction. The days begin to get longer now instead of shorter. This is also a time of giving and receiving gifts, and of joyous celebration.

So how can you use this symbolism to help you design a spread or meditation?

Here are some questions to ask yourself:

- In what area(s) have I been pulling back or holding back?

- What do I need to do or consider to stop this contraction?
  (This is provided you want to, of course!)

- Where in my life have I been experiencing darkness?
  (First define what you mean by darkness.)

- What will help me bring light into this area of my life?

- What is the greatest gift I can offer the universe at this time?

- What gift will I receive from the universe in return?

- How can I best privately celebrate this season?

- How can I best celebrate with others?

You can draw cards for these questions or others like them. Find a pattern that pleases you or meditate on them one at a time. Use your favorite deck.

Tip #62: Spread Sources

QUESTION:

Please could you tell me some alternative ways to lay out a spread? I am presently using the Celtic Cross. — Pauline

ANSWER:

Even though this is a short question, it could take a lifetime or two to answer it—there are literally thousands of ways to lay out the cards. So what I will do is point you in the direction of some excellent places to look. Pick a few spreads that appeal to you and practice them for awhile. When you feel comfortable, add a couple more to your repertory. Then a couple more, and a couple more.

The Celtic Cross is a good general reading spread, but there are many spreads that are tailored to specific topics, as you will see. It is usually my preference to be as targeted as possible when choosing a spread to answer a particular question. In fact, once you've tried out some alternatives to the Celtic Cross, you might want to design your own!

Here are a few excellent resources that should keep you and other layout "junkies" happy for a long time to come:

Websites

Ariadne's Tarot Spreads
Some of the more inventive spreads you'll come across!
http://home.mindspring.com/~ariadne1/spreads.html

Tarot Layouts FAQ V4.0
Fifty-two spreads with additional useful information.
http://www.geocities.com/Athens/2377/LayoutFAQ4.html

TarotSpreads.com
This site features over 150 spreads in nine categories along with instructions and illustrations. You can also search for spreads using any specific number of cards from 1–15.
http://www.TarotSpreads.com

Queen of Pentacles Tarot
A nice selection of illustrated spreads using six cards or more.
http://www.queenofpentacles.com/lessons/spreads/spreads. html

Wicce's Tarot Collection
The layout section of this extensive site has a good selection of spreads with clear instructions and illustrations.
http://www.wicce.com/layouts.html

Organizations

The Free Reading Network
Join this great group of people doing free three-card readings for the public and learn how to answer almost any question with three cards!
http://www.freereading.net/tarotreaders.html

Books

Classic Tarot Spreads by Sandor Konraad
Includes spreads for opening a reading—answering questions about health, love, marriage and money—as well as spreads for ending a reading.

How to Use Tarot Spreads (Llewellyn's How-To series) by Sylvia Abraham
Thirty-seven time-tested spreads that will provide the answers to the most commonly asked questions about love and romance, home and family, business and finance, major life events, and spiritual growth and past lives.

Power Tarot by Trish MacGregor & Phyllis Vega
More than 100 spreads that give specific answers to your most important questions. There are also tips on how to determine the time frame of an event, exciting insights into traditional interpretations, and easy-to-follow diagrams for the position and meaning of the cards in each spread.

Tip #63: Designing Your Own Layout

QUESTION:

How does one go about designing layouts? Why do layouts have the shapes that they do? How do you design those shapes, and figure out what the different positions mean?

I've looked through a lot of books and everyone says that of course anyone can make their own layouts, but I can't seem to get the principles from just playing around with the various types.
— Magdalena

ANSWER:

Designing my own layouts is one of my favorite Tarot practices. Wald and I have designed some together that we use to teach with but I also enjoy making them up on the spot during the course of a reading.

First of all, before you concern yourself with the shape of your layout, you'll want to define the positions. It is not always necessary to work with positions but for the purposes of this discussion, we will. After clarifying the question as best you can, take a look at the components of the question and draw a card for each component. For instance, you can draw cards to represent people, options, past events, current plans, known or unknown obstacles, potential futures, etc.

In order to determine the positions, take a good look at the question being asked. Let's use the following question as an example:

"I'm thinking of selling my crafts at an upcoming trade show. If I do, how will it go?"

Break it down into as many components as you can that describe the situation and that can help you answer the question. In this case, the factors include:

- The vendor
- Helper(s) at the booth
- The physical booth and surrounding space
- The crafts for sale
- The customers
- Income

You can simply draw a card for each consideration and lay them out one at a time, or you can get creative. Use several cards to outline a booth. These can include the cards for the booth, surrounding space and the crafts for sale. Inside the booth, place the vendor, any helpers and a cash register card. Below the booth (in front of it), choose three cards to represent the types of customers who will visit the booth.

Interpreting this spread will give a very graphic picture of all the different parts that go into the project and should do very well in answering the question.

The layout in this example is what I would call a picture layout, because it draws a picture of the scene. You can also use geometric patterns such as vertical or horizontal rows, circles, arcs, and stair-steps—a form that's particularly useful if you're trying to see how to get from Point A to Point B.

So to summarize, first find out what the question is. Then analyze the question to reveal all the components of a complete answer. Make a list of these components and assign them positions in a layout design that feels comfortable to you. Finally, interpret the cards.

This is just one approach. We recommend you read *Designing Your Own Tarot Spreads* by Teresa Michelson for more creative tools and ideas. Have fun!

FIVE

OTHER THINGS YOU CAN DO WITH TAROT

In a book devoted to practical aspects of doing readings, it is still appropriate to devote a little attention to other things you can do with Tarot. These "other things" are a bit like the unseen side of the moon. The difference is that the unseen side of the moon is a full half of what there is, and that half remains permanently hidden. But in Tarot, the other things are a lot more than half of its total lore and power, and these days they are readily available to anyone who is interested in pursuing them.

Carl Jung once said, "Your vision will become clear only when you look into your heart. Who looks outside, dreams. Who looks inside, awakens." This aspect of Tarot takes the student inside, behind closed eyes, to the universe that exists in the mind and beyond. It includes theories of creation and the nature of things, systems of magic, psychology, philosophy, symbolism and esoteric practice. It's a big place and a fascinating one although, for most people, small doses of it are quite enough. In this book, therefore, only a small amount of space is devoted to it. You'll notice that the entries in this section are not prompted by students' questions. They appeared in the *Tarot Tips* newsletter as foundation techniques for other classes we were teaching at the time. They are included here because they lead to interesting byways of Tarot that can be both useful and fun to explore.

In this section you will find a touch, a taste, of that other Tarot. The door is opened just a crack to show you some things you can do that are a little different from the common run. If you are just beginning your explorations of Tarot, they will give you a hint of how exotic this study can get. If you are an old hand at these things, you may find some interesting variations on familiar techniques, and some useful explanations to pass on to students of your own.

Tip #64: Meditation Made Easy

Before beginning a Tarot reading or study session, it's a good practice to begin with a short meditation. This will help you to relax your body and mind and simultaneously sharpen and focus your awareness. Here are two simple techniques that can be used separately or in conjunction. They work remarkably well, even for people who have difficulty meditating.

The first technique is called *Breathe and Relax*. Before you begin any kind of Tarot work, close your eyes. Breathe naturally. Observe your breath, and notice if you restrain it in any way. Relax your chest and throat. Let thoughts come and go as they will. Relax your fingers. Then relax your toes, your jaw, and your belly, in that order. Check the rest of your body for any muscular contraction and let it go. Allow your body and breath to remain relaxed for just a few minutes or for as long as you enjoy the process. When you are ready, take a deep breath and open your eyes.

Breathe and Relax is a good exercise to do whenever you are about to begin a Tarot practice, or between the parts of a complex procedure. It is also an excellent preparation for other meditations. It's very simple but wonderfully clarifying and refreshing.

The second technique is a simple three-step meditation called *The Hanged Man's Mantra,* or *Relax – Let Go – Be Still.*

- First, breathe and relax. For several breaths, pay careful attention to your in-breath—just that.

- Then, pay careful attention to your out-breath—just that.

- Finally, focus on the regular alternation of in and out breathing, and how it sustains your life.

- At this point, you will be in a meditative state.

RE–LAX: For the next few breaths, mentally repeat the word Re–Lax, saying "Re–" on the in-breath and "Lax" on the out-breath. Between each repetition, draw one breath without saying anything. Re–Lax on one breath, silence on the next breath. And as you do this, relax your body, beginning with your face and working downward. Do this three times. Re–Lax.

   Let your breathing return to normal while your body stays quite relaxed.

LET–GO: For the next few breaths, mentally repeat the words Let–Go, "Let" on the in-breath and "Go" on the out-breath, with a silent breath between each repetition. As you do this, let go of worry, anxiety or distraction, and float freely like a leaf letting go of its branch and drifting on the wind, or a raindrop merging into a pond. Do this three times. Let–Go.

   Let your breathing return to normal while you continue to float freely.

BE–STILL: For the next few breaths, mentally repeat the words Be–Still, "Be" on the in-breath and "Still" on the out-breath, with a silent breath between each repetition. As you do this, remain completely relaxed, floating freely, and become internally still and silent. Repeat this three times. Be–Still.

When you have followed these steps, you will be in a deep meditative state. Float silently and comfortably until you wish to return. The take two deep breaths, and with your eyes still closed, become completely aware of your surroundings. When you are ready, open your eyes.

Tip #65: Tarot and Meditation

> *Meditation is not anything of the mind, it is some-thing beyond the mind. And the first step is to be playful about it. If you are playful about it, mind cannot destroy your meditation. Otherwise it will turn it into another ego trip; it will make you very serious.*
>
> — Osho

Meditation is a practice that blends beautifully with the study of Tarot. It can be very playful and also yield powerful results.

We begin each live class at The Tarot School with a short meditation for several reasons:

1) It's a good way to separate ourselves from what came before—our busy day, the commute through the hectic city, etc.—and prepare ourselves for what comes next. It literally gives us some "breathing space"and helps us release our stress. This is a good thing to do in preparation for any kind of magical work and we recommend a period of meditation before any work or study with the Tarot.

2) Meditation creates sacred space in which to work. Even if you are alone, your work or reading space will be greatly enhanced by charging it with your meditation. A group meditation also creates a circle of energy among the group and helps put us all on a similar wavelength.

3. I also use the meditations in class as a teaching tool. I
   do this by designing the meditation to be a kinesthetic
   experience of the card or suit we are studying at the
   time. For instance, if we're working with the Sun, the
   meditation could be to visualize yourself lying in the
   grass on a hillside, stretched out on a blanket on the
   beach or by the pool and soaking up the heat of the sun,
   letting it relax all your muscles. This is an obvious example, but many of them get very creative and playful. The
   point is to absorb an aspect of the card through a bodily
   experience, not just intellectually or intuitively. You can
   try this on your own, too.

Here is an example of a meditation for the World card. Have
fun—play with it!

Meditation on The World Card

Tonight's class is about the World, and tonight's meditation will
be as simple as you'd like to make it or as complex as you'd like to
make it.

First take a nice, comfortable posture. Put your feet firmly on
the floor—connect with the world that you live in now. Close
your eyes and feel the connection through your feet . . .

Make a circle with your thumb and forefinger like the circle of
the wreath in the card . . .

Make a circle with your breath, going round and round . . .

Inhale through your nose . . .

Exhale through your mouth . . .

Keep the cycle going . . .

Nice and easy . . .

I'd like you to picture before you the wreath that's depicted
in the World card, standing up on its end like a doorway—

as large as a doorway. When you look at the wreath, all you will see is a swirling energy field. You cannot see what is beyond it . . .

It is not frightening. It is calming . . . and inviting . . . soothing . . . mesmerizing . . .

Beautiful light and colors . . .

In a moment, I'm going to ring the bell, and when I do, I'd like you to step through that doorway—through the wreath of the World. And you will find yourself enveloped in a state of bliss. And just breathe and relax and enjoy this state until you hear the sound of the bell again . . .

One more last long breath . . . (chime)

(continue closed-eyed meditation)

In a moment, you'll hear the sound of the bell again. And when you do, step back through the wreath, find your seat, and feel yourself in it. (chime) Once again, feel the energy of the earth connect with your feet. Send your energy down to meet it. Feel the little tingly sparks under your feet as the two energies meet and mingle . . .

Feel your knees beneath your hands, be in touch with your body, keeping your breathing steady . . .

When you're ready, gently open your eyes.

Tip #66: Contemplation

A great sage once said, "No knowledge bears fruit without contemplation." This is also true of Tarot.

Contemplation is not thinking. It is not analyzing or defining or mentally repeating conventional wisdom. No great effort is applied, and there is no specific target or goal.

Contemplation is listening and opening. It is patient and quiet. In contemplation, an image or an idea is held gently in the mind, where it is softly turned like a hard candy on the tongue so it can be observed and absorbed from different perspectives. In a short time, this gentle attention dissolves the object of contemplation in the mind, and real knowledge bubbles up into consciousness. This knowledge can be sweet, surprising, disturbing, or reassuring, but it always comes from within. It is always authentic, deeper, and truer than any conventional instruction.

Contemplating the ideas and images of Tarot opens them up and releases the sweetness of their inner meanings. This is the core technique and intention of Tarot School Study Groups. Then, by sharing our experiences with each other, each Tarot symbol that we contemplate separately becomes a pool of combined wisdom, a pool that surprises everyone by how very deep it is.

Contemplation is simple, low-tech, not demanding. But it is subtle and many-layered. Over time, if you wish, you can learn a few of its powers and go much deeper into Tarot than you ever would have guessed you could.

Tip #67: Tarot and Creative Writing

A practical use of Tarot that might not be readily apparent is the way it can aid the creative writing process. Whether you've ever tried your hand at writing or not, the cards can be used to generate ideas, flesh out a story, or help you overcome writer's block.

Next time you begin a writing project, pull out your favorite deck and ask it for suggestions. Here are some questions you might ask the cards:

- Where should my story take place? (look at the landscape)

- What should my character do next?
- What do I need to know about my character?
- How can I add a twist to the plot?
- Now my character is in trouble! How can I get him/her out?
- Should my story have a happy ending?

If you're suffering from writer's block, or perhaps even a fear of writing, use the cards to help gain some insight into your personal state. Answers to questions like these might be just what you need to get you started again:

- What is the basis of my block or fear?
- What is one action I can take to help get me past it?
- What is one more action I can take?
- Is this a good time to start a writing project? (Of course, if you're dealing with a school assignment you may not have the luxury to ask this question.)
- If not, when would be a better time to start?

Another thing you can do to help get a jump-start is to pick a single card and start "channeling" the voice of a character in the card. Get out of the way and let that character just ramble on—and write it all down! It's really an amazing process and you'll be surprised at how easy it is once you begin. It's sort of a combination Tarot reading/automatic writing session.

This is also a very good technique to use when you're trying to find the voice of a character you've already created. Look through the deck and choose a card that most closely represents the persona or energy of your character and let them speak through that card.

If you're a poet, the Tarot is an endless wellspring of inspiration. The imagery and symbolism in the cards is so rich—and there are hundreds of decks to choose from, with thousands of moods! Dive into a card and bathe in the landscape.

Don't feel you have to write a poem about the card or its meaning unless you want to. The power of the Tarot is that it can evoke from within us the most powerful feelings and experiences. Poetry is the perfect medium to express them.

According to mythology, there were nine muses. With the Tarot, you've got seventy-eight!

And that's just one deck!

Tip #68: Story Circle

The *Story Circle* is a wonderful group activity that especially lends itself to working with Tarot cards.

Each person shuffles their own deck and places it face-down in front of them. One person starts by turning over their top card and begins a story based on a character or event portrayed in the image. After about a minute (no shorter!), that person stops and the next person continues the story by turning over their top card and picking up on the sequence of events. And so it goes around the group.

There are only three rules:

1) The story must begin with "Once upon a time . . . "

2) The story must end with "And they lived happily ever after" (giving the next-to-last person the opportunity to plunge the characters into deep water!).

3) The character who is introduced in the first card must appear in every subsequent "chapter."

You can create a story circle all by yourself, using essentially the same rules as for a group. The only modification is that you must choose all the cards yourself.

First, pick the number of cards you want to use to create your story. Then, choose those cards by any method you like from a shuffled deck and lay them out face-down in a horizontal line. When all the cards are in front of you, turn over the first one and begin your story, which will, of course, be in writing. Let it take you as far as you wish, then turn the second card and continue the process. When you reach the next to the last card, it has become customary to plunge the story into its dramatic depths, and then create a happy ending with the very last card of the series.

When you are done, you will have written a wonderful, and completely unexpected, piece of fiction. This exercise can really get your creative juices flowing.

Tip #69: Determining Your Birth Cards

Knowing your birth cards is useful and important for many reasons. They are an integral part of several spreads and techniques that give you invaluable insight into your own, or anyone else's, character and destiny. For instance, **Tip #60: Year-Long Spread** is a very powerful spread/practice using your birth cards.

Please use the method described here to calculate your personal birth cards for Tarot School exercises. You may have seen it done differently elsewhere but this method is best for the specialized work we do. And we have found that the difference between this method and others produces slightly different results that most people identify with more closely.

You can determine your birth cards by doing a numerological reduction of your birth date in the following manner: MM + DD + 19* + YY. For example, let's say that your birthday is December 2, 1941. The formula would be 12 + 02 + 19 + 41 = 74. Then add

---

* For people born from January 1, 2000–December 31, 2099, the constant will be 20 instead of 19.

7 + 4 = 11. Key 11 is Justice, the first birth card for this date. 11 reduces to 2 (the High Priestess), which is the second birth card.

Here's how to handle a birth date that adds up to 3 digits. The first two digits of the three are considered as one number, which is added to the third digit. Let's look at August 20, 1969, for example. The formula would be 08 + 20 + 19 + 69 = 116. Then add 11 + 6 = 17. Key 17 is the Star, the first birth card for this date. 17 reduces to 8 (Strength), which is the second birth card. If the three numbers are 103, for example, add 10 + 3 = 13 = 4.

Almost everyone should have two birth cards. If your birth date sum reduces to a single digit (e.g. 90 = 9 + 0 = 9) the higher octave is implied (in this case, 18 – the Moon – 1 + 8 = 9). The one exception is if your birth date sum equals 19. In that case, you will have three birth cards: the Sun (19), the Wheel of Fortune (10) and the Magician (1).

Confusion about calculating birth cards is very common. Even though the math is very simple, the concept can be difficult to grasp. In case we've lost you, consider the following:

If a birthday adds up to a digit plus a zero, it reduces immediately to a single digit, but the single digits are all paired with a double digit from which it is derived. Nine, for instance, can only be arrived at, within the numbers of the Major Arcana, from the number 18 (1 + 8 = 9).

If you begin with a single digit and you search for the double digit that is its pair, you will find in most cases that there is only one possibility. There are two single digits that could have either of two double-digit pairs (3 with 12 or 21, and 2 with 11 or 20), but we have found that the first of these numbers is the one that works when beginning with a single digit sum.

9 is paired with 18 (1 + 8)　　Hermit/Moon

8 is paired with 17 (1 + 7)　　Strength/Star

7 is paired with 16 (1 + 6)　　Chariot/Tower

6 is paired with 15 (1 + 5)   Lovers/Devil

5 is paired with 14 (1 + 4)   Hierophant/Temperance

4 is paired with 13 (1 + 3)   Emperor/Death

3 is paired with 12 (1 + 2)   Empress/Hanged Man

2 is paired with 11 (1 + 1)   High Priestess/Justice

1 is paired with 10 (1 + 0)   Magician/Wheel of Fortune

If your birthdate sum = 21, it reduces to 3, so the World is paired with the Empress. If your birthdate sum equals 20, it reduces to 2, so Judgement is paired with the High Priestess.

Again, there is one exception where you will have three birth cards. If your birth date sum = 19, it will reduce first to 19, then to 10, and finally 1 – Sun/Wheel/Magician.

If the subject intrigues you, The Tarot School has a comprehensive audio course on understanding and working with birth card sets.

Tip #70: Tarot Persona

Ever wish you could practice reading for new people but the only people you know well enough to practice on are those you've already read for a hundred times? Here's a fun technique you can try with a partner or in a group:

Have the person you're reading for create a persona. Just like in a play or role-gaming adventure, their persona should be as multidimensional as they can imagine. Your partner should be able to describe their character, know their history, and feel their emotions. What kind of problem would their character have that would bring them to a reader? Let your partner, as the persona, ask a question and respond to your reading in character.

Conduct your reading session just as if you were reading for a real person. This is excellent practice and can be great fun at a party!

Tip #71: Tarot and Coping

When facing a particularly stressful time, there are a number of ways that Tarot can help us cope. Here are a few techniques designed to dispel the feeling of helplessness and anxiety:

- **Card-A-Day Variation**
  If you are in the habit of drawing a card each morning (or if you are planning to begin this practice), instead of picking a card at random, consciously choose a card whose qualities you wish to work with that day. This could be a happy card to help combat depression, a card that gives you strength in overcoming fear, or a card such as the 3 of Swords or 5 of Cups that might allow you space to grieve. If anger is what you need to release, choose a card that expresses this for you. You may wish to choose a second card suggesting a way you can channel that anger that is not harmful.

  Choosing, rather than drawing a card at random, can give you a tool for making proactive responses to difficult situations. By doing this, you take more control over how you lead your life and remove the more reactive focus of predictive readings.

- **10 of Cups Meditation**
  You may be aware that the 10 of Cups (in the *Waite-Smith/Universal Waite* deck) is considered a stage card. If you look at the image you'll notice that the people are standing on a flat surface that is separated from the background by a horizontal line. Because of that, this card can be interpreted as a false sense of happiness—

a make-believe play where the real events are happening
behind the scenes. Recently, I have come to see another
way of using the backdrop aspect of this card that can
be a very powerful tool.

Consider, instead, that through the power of their
own hearts (Cups), the people in the card are envisioning, invoking, and manifesting the happy scene. They are
bringing it into existence by projecting their loving
vision onto the scrim of their universe. Use this intention of the 10 of Cups to help you focus your own meditation or magical working. You can choose an additional
card or cards that represent peace, safety, cooperation or
whatever you wish to envision, to add power to your
work.

- **Action Card**
  Choose one card, either consciously or at random, that
  will tell you the next thing to actually *do*. In the spirit of
  taking things one step at a time, do not choose another
  card until you have taken that action. If you have been
  having problems with motivation, this could help.

- **Tarot Role-play**
  When we experience trauma or powerful emotions, a
  common response is to repress our feelings. While this
  might be useful in the short term, it can be counter-
  productive in the long run. Tarot role-playing is a thera-
  peutic technique that can be used with adults and children alike, alone or with another person.

  Choose a card and write or speak as the character in
  the card. How would *they* express their feelings about
  what has happened? What would *they* do? You might
  want to tape record this exercise. It can be powerful,
  and if it is, you'll learn something valuable by listening
  to it later.

Because Tarot is a mirror, ultimately everything you say or write is coming from you, but oftentimes we have trouble expressing intense feelings and this exercise might help you with that.

- **Create A Tarot Prayer Mandala**
  Consciously choose five cards that visually represent your personal prayer for yourself, your loved ones, your community, and/or the world. Lay them out as a square of four cards with a space in the center. Place the fifth card in the center. Leave some room between the cards for the energy of the mandala to circulate.

  If you like, you can assign the four Elements and Spirit to the positions if you are comfortable with working that way. Use this mandala as a focus for your prayers or meditation. Leave it out for at least twenty-four hours.

If you give it some thought, you can probably come up with a number of other ways that you can use Tarot for emotional support. I must say, however, that these methods should not replace professional psychological care if that's what you need.

SIX

ETHICS

O ver the years, Ruth Ann and I have found that experienced Tarot readers generally fall into three broad
categories. There is the strong reader, the good reader, and the great reader. The difference between them is a
subtle combination of factors.

The strong reader has lots of native talent—a blend of
psychic ability, life experience, an intuitive feel for the
cards, shrewd understanding of peoples' emotional states
and problems, and a self-confident style. Formal knowledge and skill are add-ons—good, but not necessary. A
sense of ethics may be irrelevant to strong readers since it
does nothing to enhance their personal image or con-
tribute to their personal success. There have been, over the
centuries, an army of strong readers, with varying amounts
of knowledge and skill and no ethics whatever. It is this
group that has done the most to give Tarot its persistently
bad reputation with the general public. Readers like these,
though clearly competent, are defined by their use of Tarot
as a tool to serve themselves, and range from the insensi-
tive through the manipulative to the criminal.

The *good* reader need have only a modest talent plus
reasonable knowledge and skill. In this context, "good"
means the ability to be both effective and helpful. It means
leaving a querent better off at the end of a reading than at

the beginning. It means the ability to create a genuine and lasting satisfaction for the querent. Good readers help to counteract the harm done to Tarot's reputation by the strong but unethical ones.

A *great* reader combines talent, knowledge, skill and ethics into an awesome combination, and *you* can become a great reader if you wish. Maximize your talent by bringing together and focusing all your abilities, experience, powers of observation, sensitivity, and empathy. Learn and practice continuously, and always keep your querent's best interests at the center of your attention.

Focusing on your querent's best interests is easily the most subtle and most difficult of divinatory skills. To be truly sensitive to the needs of each querent; to be compassionate, delicate, and skillful; to be deeply helpful and carefully avoid the damage that can be caused by blundering; this is the function of ethics in Tarot. This is what really separates a great reader from the rest.

In this last section, we broach the issue of ethics in reading. This is another area of Tarot that deserves a book of its own, though we only have room here to touch on the subject. As usual, we answer questions from our students and bring up things we think you'll find useful and would like to know.

Tip #72: Bad News

One of your goals as a reader should be, as much as possible, to leave the querent feeling better at the end of their reading than when they started. Does this mean you should never give bad news?

No, but you should be very careful how you discuss difficult issues and challenges with your client. Chances are, if they are going through a tough time or someone close to them is very ill, for example, telling them this will *not* come as a surprise. The best thing to do, however, is not to dwell on the trouble but discover things that the querent can actually do about their situation.

One of the best ways to achieve this is to end the reading session with an *Action Card*. This card will suggest a concrete action that the querent can take that will help their situation. It may involve others or it may simply be a way that they can nurture themselves until their difficulty ends. Not every situation can be changed, but sometimes just having something constructive to do in the meantime can be a great anxiety reliever.

Tip #73: The Death Card

QUESTION:

My name is Vanja and I am from the Netherlands. I am just starting Tarot, and have a question about the Death card. I have two books about Tarot and some info off the Internet. In one of the books the Death card means physical death and in the other, the ending of a situation, etc. Can it mean physical death? Because some say you can't predict death with Tarot. — Vanja

ANSWER:

It's been our experience that you can predict anything with Tarot. Ask a question and Tarot will answer it, whatever it is. That doesn't mean that you don't need to use tact, delicacy, and understanding when answering a question as difficult and sensitive as one concerning death.

Strictly speaking, the Death card in Tarot refers to irrevocable change. That can be interpreted in different ways according to the question. There are situations in which the appearance of the Death card in a reading would certainly suggest physical death. It does happen, after all.

However, in the vast majority of cases, the issue does not concern a physical death but more likely a radical and transformative change.

Let me tell you about two different readings that I actually did.

In the first, a woman came to me for a reading when I was working in a metaphysical shop. She was a stranger who was clearly troubled. She told me that she was waiting for the results of a biopsy, and cancer was a definite possibility. She wanted to know what the results would show. I drew three cards face-down and turned them over one at a time. I did it fairly quickly so all three got turned over before she could express a reaction. The middle card was Death. The woman did not wait for an explanation but ran sobbing from the table. She read the card herself.

In another case, a mature man who came to me for a private reading complained that he didn't know what to do next—life was stale, his plans had run into brick walls, and there wasn't anything he really wanted to do. He was without direction and there was no "taste" in his life. He wanted to know when this condition would end, if ever. I did a six-month calendar spread just to see if things would open up by themselves. The sixth card was Death and it came at the end of a succession of difficult and stormy cards. The answer here was that this man's life would undergo a dramatic change and things would never be the same. Definitely life would open up. The blockage would be removed.

The two cases are radically different. Moving on, truly changing on a deep level is often frightening but sometimes it's just what you need.

So all of your sources are at least partially correct, even though they seem contradictory. The interpretation always depends on the context.

Tip #74: Asking About Others

QUESTION:

Lately I've been wondering about the information the Tarot gives when I ask questions about other people. Specifically, questions like "How does John feel about Jean?" or "Is John a trustworthy person?" "What do I need to know about John as a suitable partner?" etc. I've begun wondering if the cards are reflecting how the querent views John.

For example, if the querent believes John is not a trustworthy person and the Knight of Wands, reversed comes up, are the cards reflecting how the querent views John or are the cards reflecting some aspect of John? Is there a way to distinguish this in readings (particularly when doing single-card readings)? Should I not be asking such questions? — Susan

ANSWER:

This is actually a very complicated issue. In short, to answer your basic concern, the cards will answer the question asked. However, the difficulty comes from the possibility of projection, since the reader will normally see things from the perspective of the querent. This means that the reader has to be especially careful to be objective and see all the possibilities in a case like this. And there are no guarantees. The best safeguard against projection is a very carefully framed question.

As far as the appropriateness of answering third-party questions—avoid them if you possibly can. There is a big issue of invasion of privacy here. The best approach is always to ask questions from the point of view of the querent, as they involve the querent. For example, "Would John make a good partner for me?"

"How does John feel about Jean?" is definitely a question you should not attempt to answer. Neither party is present and it's not ethical to spy on them through a reading. If Jean happens to be the querent, however, she could reasonably ask, "How does John feel about me?" Ideally, the querent should be at the center of every question.

Tip #75: Reading for Children

QUESTION:

I was wondering if you could give us your insight on whether a Tarot reader should or should not do readings for children (on the child's request, not at the request of the parents who want to know something about their children).

Before asking you, I've asked many professionals in my country (France) and gotten a different answer from each person. I would love to have your point of view. — Frédérique

ANSWER:

This is a fascinating issue and touches on a subtle aspect of reading.

In order to read for anyone, you need to share a common language (and I don't mean French or English). You need to share a vocabulary, not only of words and phrases, but ideas and experiences.

As you are probably well aware, children often see things differently than adults do. Their premises are not necessarily the same as ours. What is real for a very young child, we often regard as imagination or foolishness. At every age, a child acquires new levels of understanding and a new vocabulary of shared experience.

If you, as a reader, feel that you and the child for whom you are reading can understand each other (this has to go *both ways*), I don't see any reason why you couldn't do a useful reading for that child. In my experience, however, not many people can do that.

I generally include myself among those who don't do this very well, but recently I had the occasion to do a one-card reading for each of two young sisters. In both cases, the readings were remarkably appropriate and very well-received by the children themselves. In fact, both of them had big grins of recognition and appreciation on their faces when I had finished.

But I see a risk in reading for a child. Children are extremely impressionable and they do not have our mental or emotional defenses. If what a reader says makes a strong impression, then that impression will be taken to heart. A strong impression can be made even when what is said is a mistake—and we all make mistakes. So be careful, because there are more potential consequences in reading for a child than for an adult.

That said, use your own judgment. You may find it changes from case to case.

Tip #76: Predicting Life Span

QUESTION:

Last week, a Hungarian friend of mine asked me if the Tarot could predict the age limit of a person. Intuitively I sensed that this is a question that demands a level of precision in the answer that the Tarot is not generally designed for. Nor have I come across any Tarot spread that has been documented to address this issue. However, I realized that a common expectation of divination (or "fortunetelling") from the lay person is to be able to find out how long he or she can live.

If you do encounter a querent with this question, how would you approach it? — Peter

ANSWER:

This is rather a complex issue, Peter, which can be addressed from a couple of different perspectives.

Since you mentioned the issue of precision, let's start there. I would tend to agree that Tarot is not reliably precise when it comes to long-term predictions, but that doesn't mean that it never is. I think that kind of precision has a lot to do with the particular psychic/intuitive talents of the reader. It's probably not impossible to make such a prediction, but there's certainly no foolproof formula for being consistently correct, so, personally, I would be very skeptical about predictions about life span.

The exception to this is when the reading concerns someone who is terminally ill. In a shorter time-frame like that, a calendar spread or other method for determining timing may very well give you this kind of information.

The other side to this question, however, is how appropriate it is to answer it in the first place. Again, speaking for myself, the only time that I would consider addressing the question of life-span is when dealing with someone who is critically ill where plans need to be made to get this person's affairs in order. Even here, there is still no guarantee of accuracy and old-fashioned common sense, along with the doctor's prognosis, would probably be more useful than a Tarot reading. The reading can be more valuable by addressing the querent's issues and needs instead.

As far as predicting lifespan out of curiosity or "for entertainment purposes," I wouldn't do it. There's a Sanskrit word, *samskara*, which is similar to the English word, *scar*. Essentially, it refers to a karmic groove that is carved into our etheric being when significant events happen or statements are made that leave an impression. These samskaras, which are usually carried with us for years, even lifetimes, are said to be at the root of all our problems.

If you were to attempt a lifespan reading and the answer you got was that the person would die young, consider the emotional ramifications of such a statement. It would probably color the rest of that person's life, even if they weren't sure they believed you. Except in rare circumstances, to answer this question serves no useful purpose and has the potential to cause a lot of harm.

So if anyone asked that question of me, I would simply tell them I don't do that kind of reading. There's no law that says you have to answer every question that's asked.

Tip #77: Going Pro

QUESTION:

When do you think a person is ready to become a professional Tarot reader? And how do you go about doing it?

I have been studying the cards for about three years. I do readings for myself all the time. I do it for my friends. I enjoy doing it and would like to branch out and perhaps gain an income from it, so any insight is welcomed. — Michelle

ANSWER:

There are several things that are, in my opinion, requirements before taking money from the public for readings. Unfortunately, there are many "professional" readers out there who don't follow these guidelines and I believe that's where Tarot as a profession runs into trouble.

Know the Cards

This may seem obvious, but people who are impatient to earn money reading Tarot often begin before they know very much at all. So what exactly do I mean by this?

First of all, before you can legitimately call yourself a professional, you need to have a comfortable familiarity with several different interpretations for all seventy-eight cards, preferably on more than one level. By this I mean to include psychological as well as standard divinatory interpretations, and if possible, some esoteric meanings as well. The sign of comfortable familiarity is that you are able to remember and use these meanings without referring to a book or notebook.

You can develop this familiarity through a combination of:

- Formal study with a teacher, school, or association
- Continually reading good books on different aspects of Tarot
- Participating in online discussion groups
- Personal meditation
- Reading for friends, family, and fellow students
- Collecting interpretations offered through automated readings

Take notes, make lists, keep a journal, and practice, practice, practice!

Decide how you feel about reading reversals. If you don't wish to use them, make sure you know the full spectrum of meanings contained in each card so that when difficult situations arise you can recognize them and advise your querent appropriately. Do I mean that if you ever draw a blank during a reading you can't be a pro? No. Ask anyone who's been reading for twenty-plus years and they'll tell you it happens from time to time—even to them. For some effective techniques on how to handle blanking out, see **Tip #41: Drawing a Blank**.

Know a Variety of Spreads

Wean yourself off the Celtic Cross and learn some spreads that target the question better. There are several excellent books on spreads (see our recommended book list), and the Internet is a large and growing resource. Two fine sources of spreads on the internet can be found here:

- **TarotSpreads.com**
  http://www.TarotSpreads.com

- **Tarot Layouts FAQ V4.0**
  http://www.geocities.com/Athens/2377/LayoutFAQ4.html

See **Tip #62: Spread Sources** for more resource suggestions.

Practice designing your own spreads. I find that many times the best spread to use for a particular reading is one that is created on the spot and customized for the question asked. See **Tip #63: Designing Your Own Layout** for tips on how to approach creating your own spreads.

Have a Code of Ethics

Even if you don't publish your code of ethics, know what you can do and what you can't. Know what you will do and what you won't. Take some time to think about how you can best serve the public. Use this opportunity to determine what's important to you and to define your personal style of reading. For suggestions, take a look at what others have written. You can often find personal codes of ethics on the websites of other professional readers. Go to45Google.com or another favorite search engine and type the following:

"Code of Ethics" and tarot

You'll have all the samples you could wish for.

Here are some standard guidelines you might want to consider when constructing your own code:

1. **Honest Dealings**
   Promise to avoid shady practices, or even the appearance
   of such practices. These typically include pressuring
   clients for return visits; offering to remove hexes or curs-
   es, or to pray for them; or offering any service other than
   a reading in return for money.

2. **Prediction Policy and Belief**
   Know what you believe about prediction with Tarot,
   what you can and can't do, and will or won't do, and let
   the client know these things before you agree to do a
   reading.

3. **Limits of Expertise**
   Clearly and carefully avoid giving professional advice
   unless you are legally qualified to do so. This includes
   medical, legal, financial, psychological, or any other
   licensed or regulated kinds of advice.

4. **Third-Party Readings**
   The subject of a reading should always be the querent.
   Don't do readings about the actions, thoughts, or feelings of anyone not present unless they are in connection
   with the querent. This is an invasion of privacy. (See **Tip
   #74: Asking About Others.**)

5. **Delicacy**
   Treat every querent and their personal issues seriously.
   Always be tactful, and when bad news or unpleasant
   matters come up in a reading, tell the truth, but avoid
   creating unnecessary pain with undue bluntness. (See
   Tip #72: Bad News.)

6. **Compassion**
   Treat every querent with love and respect, and avoid
   injecting personal judgments into your readings. Be
   aware that your personal judgments are always your own
   issues and not your querent's.

7. **Dependency**
Never tell clients what to do. Encourage them to make their own decisions. Do not encourage them to rely on frequent readings for continual guidance. Never take advantage of a querent's emotional, physical, or financial vulnerability.

8. **Confidentiality**
Maintain total confidentiality about all readings, unless someone may come to personal harm through your silence, or criminality is involved.

9. **Knowledge**
Commit yourself to continual learning and personal growth. Read from your own highest state. In every reading, invoke your own highest wisdom, understanding, and knowledge.

10. **Client Satisfaction**
Make your very best effort in every reading to answer your querents' questions, provide them with useful insights and information, and leave them happier, wiser, and more empowered than when you began.

Whatever you choose to include in your own personal code should reflect your beliefs and be an accurate description of what a client can expect from you as a reader.

Know Your Local Laws

Every state, county, and city in America, and, I'm sure, the equivalent governmental bodies in other countries, have either laws or policies regarding fortunetelling and readers of all kinds. If you want to do readings professionally, you really need to know what these are before you hang out your shingle.

Sometimes, for example, Tarot reading may be condoned by your state, but prohibited by your town or county. Occasionally, a special license may be required to do readings in your area. The fees for such a license can be, and often are intended to be, prohibitively expensive. Restrictive statutes can be and have been overturned through public opinion and activism, and if you are inclined to be proactive, you can help the cause of Tarot in this way.

Acquire Credentials

Professional credentials convey to your clients that you are serious and knowledgeable and will help allay any fears they may have that you're trying to rip them off.

Reputable Tarot schools, teachers, and organizations in America and abroad often offer a variety of courses of study that lead to internal degrees or some type of professional certification. When choosing an organization or teacher for the degree or certificate they offer, be sure to do your research. Most are legitimate, but some are questionable.

Determine Your Fee

Tarot readers charge anywhere from an open donation to $200+ for a reading. Set your own fee based on:

- Your level of experience
- Your geographical location
- What the majority of other readers in your area are charging
- Your personal comfort level

If you develop a steady clientele, it will be difficult to raise your rates, so don't charge a lower fee than you feel you're worth just because you're starting out. Keep in mind that you want to establish a fair exchange of energy and charge accordingly.

Attend to the Practicalities

Once you have done your best to prepare for your new career as a professional reader, there are still a whole lot of practical details you'll need to attend to in order to make your business a success. Things like business cards, advertising, preparing your space, building and keeping your clientele, etc.

For comprehensive information on these and many other details, we recommend Christine Jette's book, *Professional Tarot: The Business of Reading, Consulting & Teaching* (Llewellyn Worldwide, Ltd., 2003).

Now that I've said all that, one of the most important things to do, as far as I'm concerned, is to read for others with an open heart. Read professionally because you have something to offer others—not because you need something from them. Tarot is a spiritual path and helping others by becoming a professional reader can be an important part of that path. If you feel a call in that direction, honor its power.

I've spent all this time discussing a few of the considerations that go into making you a professional reader. But—and this is a big but—there are other ways to be a Tarot professional.

Several of the best-known and most beloved of our Tarot colleagues, people who earn all or much of their living from Tarot, do so by writing books, creating decks, publishing books and decks, teaching and lecturing, and establishing professional Tarot organizations. Reading professionally is often an adjunct to these endeavors, but not always. Each of these ways of being a Tarot professional has its own very high standards of achievement, and its own special business requirements.

Over time, Tarot as a profession has grown in subtlety and complexity and will surely continue to do so. If you want to be a pro, learn continually, practice constantly, and be guided by love of what you do.

AFTERWORD

Tip #78: Heretical Musings

The Diamond Sutra says:
"the past is ungraspable,
the present is ungraspable,
the future is ungraspable."
so what the hell are you doing?
Live now, be what you are
and enjoy, enjoy, yet again enjoy.
— Ti Shan

I have to say that when it really comes down to it, I share this philosophy. Not that I'm all that good at living it (yet), but I'm working on it. From time to time, I'll discuss something going on in my life with someone and they'll ask me, "What did the cards say about it?" or "Did you do a reading on it?" Almost always, my answer is "No."

Now, many of you may feel those are pretty strange words for a Tarot reader/teacher/author—especially someone who is devoting her life's work to it. After all, isn't the Past-Present-Future spread one of the most basic, popular, and important aspects of working with the Tarot?

- Basic? — absolutely.

- Popular? — sure.

- Important? — well . . .

I suppose that really depends upon your personal approach to things. Tarot is certainly a fine tool for looking at our daily lives and all its past, present, and future details. And there are certainly times when gaining perspective in difficult or confusing times is extremely valuable. I just don't think it's a good idea to get hooked on this type of reading. There are people I know who practically can't leave the house without doing a reading to see what's going on. What happens, in my opinion, is that they cease to trust their own judgment about even simple things. This is not good.

I'm not referring to the practice of pulling a Card-a-Day. This can be a very useful tool for learning the cards, gaining insight about yourself, or familiarizing yourself with a new deck. It's interesting to see, in retrospect, how your day corresponds with the symbols in the card. However, even here, there is some danger if you allow the card to influence your mood or actions before the day has even begun.

Predictive readings can be a set-up. They have the capacity to rob of us our own spontaneous experience of life. Does that mean I'm against them? Not really. Will I do predictive readings? Sure, if it's appropriate. I just don't usually do them for myself. (Neither does Wald, by the way.)

So how can you use Tarot to "live now, be what you are, and enjoy, enjoy, yet again enjoy?"

There are lots of ways, actually. Tarot is a mirror which can show us the magical beings we are. It's a never-ending source of wonder and delight with something for everyone—history, art, magic, psychology. I find correlations within Tarot to my personal spiritual path and use it to help me gain a higher understanding of my world.

It's fun! You can use it to play games and it's one of the best tools I know of for inspiring creativity and beating writer's block. You can jump into a Tarot landscape and have endless adventures. You can commune with the characters, experience their wisdom, and bring it back with you. I could go on and there are, I'm sure, many delicious uses for Tarot that haven't even been dreamed of yet.

So if you've noticed a tendency to rely on the cards as a constant reality-check, or if you find yourself getting caught up in trying to grasp the "ungraspable" past, present, or future, let it go for awhile. Explore some of the other ways Tarot can help enrich your life so you can "live now" and "be what you are."

Enjoy!

— Ruth Ann Amberstone

RECOMMENDED BOOKS

There are quite a number of good Tarot books currently on the market. Here is a basic list of some that we recommend to our students:

For a clear, thorough explanation of how to read Tarot, for beginners:

- Joan Bunning: *Learning the Tarot*

For a broad look at techniques and interpretations:

- Mary K. Greer: *Tarot For Your Self*
- Rachel Pollack: *Seventy-Eight Degrees of Wisdom*

Rich resources for spreads:

- Evelin Burger & Johannes Fiebig: *The Complete Book of Tarot Spreads*
- Sandor Konraad: *Classic Tarot Spreads*
- Trish MacGregor & Phyllis Vega: *Power Tarot*

For an historical overview:

- Michael Dummett: *A History of the Occult Tarot: 1870–1970*

- Cynthia Giles: *The Tarot: History, Mystery and Lore*
- Stuart Kaplan: *The Encyclopedia of Tarot* (several volumes)

For more advanced students interested the esoteric aspects of Tarot:

- Israel Regardie: *The Golden Dawn*
- Robert Wang: *The Qabalistic Tarot*

For intermediate/advanced students and Tarot professionals of all kinds:

- Llewellyn's *Special Topics in Tarot* series. This series was especially created to fill the needs of experienced students, readers, and teachers. Each book takes an in-depth look at a different aspect of Tarot practice. Collect them all.

Other favorites include:

- Geraldine Amaral & Nancy Cunningham: *Tarot Celebrations: Honoring the Inner Voice*
- Paul Foster Case: *Book of Tokens —Tarot Meditations*
- Lon Milo DuQuette: *The Chicken Qabalah of Rabbi Lamed Ben Clifford*
- Mary K. Greer: *The Complete Book of Tarot Reversals*
- Marcia Masino: *The Easy Tarot Guide*
- Jason C. Lotterhand: *The Thursday Night Tarot*
- Rachel Pollack: *The Complete Illustrated Guide to Tarot*

Go to Amazon.com and do a search on "Tarot." They have an extensive inventory of books with descriptive blurbs and reader reviews which may help in your decision-making process.

You can also visit other Tarot sites that publish book reviews. There are many that do, but starting here should keep you pretty busy:

- **Tarot Passages —www.TarotPassages.com**

- **Wicce's Tarot Collection — www.wicce.com**

The Tarot is, above all, a vehicle for symbolic imagery. These symbols may be interpreted in many different ways. Symbols that have their origin with the Golden Dawn and other mystical orders are to be interpreted within the system of Western Hermeticism. However, those same symbols, as well as other pictorial images, can be interpreted purely intuitively. What do they make you think of?

Another way to interpret the symbology found in Tarot is to look beyond Tarot books at sources of general symbolism. There are many excellent symbol dictionaries on the market, along with other books that give some attention to symbol interpretation. Here are some of the symbolism books that we have on our shelf; there are many more:

- Tom Chetwind: *Dictionary of Symbols*

- Jean Chevalier, Alain Gheerbrant: *The Penguin Dictionary of Symbols*

- J. E. Cirlot: *A Dictionary of Symbols*

- David Fontana: *The Secret Language of Symbols*

- Barbara Walker: *The Woman's Dictionary of Symbols & Sacred Objects*

Also, there are publishers, such as Thames and Hudson, that publish books on specialized topics that will have symbolic references in them as well. You might want to check out their *Sacred Symbols* series. They are tiny books which are beautifully produced and have a wealth of information.

Then, of course, if you're looking for a complete reference of all the symbolism found in the *Rider-Waite-Smith* deck, there's our own *Tarot School Correspondence Course*. As far as we know, there is no other single source for card-by-card interpretations of all the symbols in both the Major and Minor Arcana.

In addition to Tarot-specific books, and books on general symbolism, there is a wealth of general esoteric literature that has a direct bearing on the root of meaning in Tarot. Some favorites that we have found very useful, accessible, and enjoyable are:

- Aryeh Kaplan, Sefer Yetzirah: *The Book of Creation*

- W. Kirk Macnulty: *Freemasonry: A Journey Through Ritual and Symbol*

- Adam McLean: *The Alchemical Mandala*

On the general subject of Tarot books, the last word should be a caution. Tarot literature is already so extensive that we can't keep up with it. New books on Tarot keep pouring off the presses and it is quite possible, we think, to drown in information overload. So we have provided only a very short list of books we know personally and can comfortably recommend. These books are all fairly simple and straightforward and we're sure that anyone who hasn't read them already will find them useful.

But everyone's needs and tastes are different, and our final recommendation is that you head for your nearest bookstore, follow your nose and read what looks like fun. Dive into Tarot literature the way you would dive into cool water on a hot day, and enjoy it immensely!

THE TAROT SCHOOL STORY

The Tarot School was born on February 1, 1995 and, just as with a human being, its development and growth has been an exciting and constantly evolving process. Many people have asked us if there is a Tarot School in their area, or have considered creating something similar and asked our advice in getting started. By sharing the story of the school so far, we hope to give you an idea of what raising "our baby" has been like.

Bonus Tips for Tarot Business

Perhaps you'd like to start your own school someday and can learn from our successes and mistakes. If not, we at least hope you'll find our experiences entertaining.

In the Beginning . . .

Back in the twentieth century (the Winter of 1994 to be exact), we were hanging out with our friends Irene Kendall and Lelia Dickerson at The Open Center, a wholistic learning center in SoHo. Although the four of us are very different, we all share one thing—a love of Tarot.

On this particular evening we were discussing how, although we knew of occasional one-day or weekend workshops on Tarot, and even a six-week introductory course or two, there was nowhere to study Tarot in New York City on a continuing basis—no place where one could study the cards in-depth. If you went to a class, there was only enough time to spend a few minutes on each card. After that, except for a few good books, you were on your own. The Tarot community as we know it now didn't exist at the time.

"Wouldn't it be great if there were someplace we could meet to study Tarot every week," asked Irene. "Someplace where we could take time with the cards?"

Not being content to just talk, we made plans to change this sorry state of affairs, and a couple of months later, The Tarot School opened its doors.

The two of us made the commitment to lead a weekly three-hour class at the Source of Life Center in midtown, and Lelia and Irene agreed to come as often as they could to help out. We put out a flyer at the Source of Life, bought an ad in a local New Age newspaper, and waited for a flood of students.

At first, there were only two or three students each week. The truth is, there were a couple of times when nobody came at all. But optimism, patience, and perseverance eventually paid off, and The Tarot School grew in surprising ways.

Nine years later, weekly classes are still going strong. Our students love being able to spend a full two hours or more discussing a card and then having the chance to practice and exchange readings. Numerous lasting friendships have been formed in class as well. We're proud of the many students who have earned a Tarot School degree; they have become confident and competent professional readers, whether or not they read for the public.

Bonus Tip

- Identify a need and find a way to meet it

Developing a Teaching Style

From the beginning, we made the decision to teach a mixed-level class. Just because someone is first starting their studies, we reasoned, doesn't mean they're not intelligent enough to follow classes that would be of interest to more experienced students. Everyone starts at the deep end of the pool, and nobody has drowned yet.

Every year we vary our approach to the cards. (We take a full year to cover the entire deck.) This keeps our own interest level up, as well as the interest of those students who continue to take classes for several years. Students come and go throughout the year, but there is usually a core group who attend most of the time. This core group shifts every once in awhile, and one thing we've noticed is that each group has its own preferred way of learning. Some enjoy practical classes with experiential techniques, while others would rather have every last bit of information we can give them to put in their notebooks. We try to keep the material balanced while remaining sensitive to the changing needs of our student body. If you're teaching a short-term course with a set curriculum, this is not so important, but if you're considering ongoing classes, it's a good idea to keep your teaching style flexible.

Bonus Tips

- Determine your approach, your teaching style, and what you want to offer

- Develop an interesting and balanced learning experience

- Stay flexible enough to continually respond to student/client feedback and continually improve your classes/services

Getting Graphic

One of our most valuable properties is our logo. It's a beautiful graphic representation of the four suit symbols that we must have used in about a hundred different ways by now. David Heizer, an excellent illustrator, designed it for us, and we owe him a debt of gratitude for the gift.

A logo is the best way to represent yourself to the public, even if it's just a special graphic treatment of your name. If you want your logo to include a pictorial element, avoid the clipart and have a custom drawing created just for you. This will help identify you as unique.

Bonus Tips

- Have a clear vision of the image you want to present
- Have a professional create a logo to express that vision
- Keep your image professional

Arcanum

Arcanum magazine was a labor of love which we started in 1996 and published for a little over two years. Although the publication included Tarot content, it was more of a contemporary journal of occult writing and thought, and included a whole range of magical topics.

As with other large projects we occasionally undertake, we had no idea what life-consuming effort it would take to put together and print a graphically intensive publication, cultivate a stable of writers, sell advertising, deal with distributors and fulfill subscriptions. And we published *Arcanum* every two months!

As hard as it was to give up, there came a point where we had to decide whether we were going to devote our energies to developing new programs for The Tarot School, or to keeping the magazine going. Eventually, in a meditation, Ruth Ann got the message to drop it. This has definitely turned out for the best; we have been able to deepen and expand our work considerably, and keep the focus exclusively on Tarot.

Bonus Tips

- Try new things

- Be willing to let go of things that don't work

- Don't spread your resources, including your time, too thin

Be There or Be Square

While visiting a Manhattan metaphysical shop in 1997, we picked up a brochure for an upcoming event that we just couldn't miss. The International Tarot Society (a group we'd never heard of before) was hosting a World Tarot Congress that October, in Chicago, Illinois. Over twenty authors and teachers would be presenting workshops—every one of them about Tarot!

People from all over the world attended what was essentially the birth of the modern Tarot community. We met, and began long-term relationships with, colleagues and students alike. These connections have led to ventures we could never have foreseen at the time (including this book!). Networking at Tarot conferences and events is one of the strongest pieces of advice we can offer anyone who is interested in developing a public Tarot career. The contacts you'll make at these events are invaluable—and they are a tremendous amount of fun!

The 1997 World Tarot Congress was the first of many Tarot conferences to be presented by the ITS and other groups and individuals. We've had the privilege to teach at a number of them, and ultimately began producing Tarot events of our own. But that's another story...

Bonus Tips

- Network and be part of the Tarot community
- Attend local, regional, and national conferences
- Participate in on-line communities

"T-Shirts"

There was a time when we had the bright idea to create and sell a line of t-shirts with Tarot cards on them. We thought the public would love to wear some of the fabulous art that can be found in Tarot decks, and that we could add a profitable income stream to our business. We had contacts with owners of metaphysical stores who were already selling issues of *Arcanum*, and we knew a guy who was willing to produce the t-shirts in small quantities. We obtained the necessary licensing agreements for a large set of images, set up a separate bookkeeping procedure to handle fees and royalties, found a vendor of quality shirts, and designed the necessary sell-sheets and order forms. Then we spent a lot of time running around taking and filling orders—all in person. Because they knew us, the shop owners bought them.

There were two major problems with this venture. The first was that the public (for whatever reason) did *not* buy them, and we probably spent more money than we made. But more important-ly, we discovered that an even bigger problem was that in order to be successful at selling t-shirts, we needed to learn about, and be in, the t-shirt business. Our purpose is to teach Tarot, not sell clothing, and we had lost sight of that.

Over the years, it's been very tempting to get into all kinds of side ventures but our experience has taught us that many of them are just another version of t-Shirts. The trick has been to recognize when that's the case and not waste our time, money, and energy on anything that is not integral to our purpose.

Bonus Tip

- Develop a mission statement for your business and stick to it

Reaching Out

One of the features of *Arcanum* magazine was a regular column on card study called "Notes from The Tarot School." This column began as a series of notes we prepared for some of our classes on the Major Arcana. When we decided to reach out to students who didn't live close enough to attend our live classes, we began the long process of expanding on these notes to create a correspondence course.

We wanted the course to include the complete symbolism of the visual imagery in the *Rider-Waite-Smith* deck, and discovered that this material was scattered all over the available literature in bits and pieces. Many months of research, thinking, integrating, writing, and typesetting went into the preparation process. In 1998 the *Tarot School Correspondence Course* was launched. It has since been enjoyed by Tarot enthusiasts all over the globe, and we went from being local teachers to an "international company."

We'll let you in on a little secret. The course was only half-finished when those first lessons were mailed. We fully expected that we'd be able to complete writing it in the next six months, but it wound up taking much longer than we'd planned, so we wrote an interim review lesson at the mid-point in the course, and created the concept of the one-month hiatus between the later lessons. Originally, we thought we'd remove the hiatus periods once the course was completed, but we got so much feedback from people thanking us for giving them these breaks, we decided to leave them in. So now you know the real reason why you'll receive the twelve lessons over a period of sixteen months!

Bonus Tips

- Remember that sometimes a little faith goes a long way

- When things don't go according to plan, see if you can turn a potentially negative situation into a positive one

Web Weaving

At the same time that we were working on the course (while still teaching), it became apparent that we needed an internet presence. Ruth Ann taught herself basic HTML in order to design our website, and the initial process took about six months. Admittedly, the code is pretty primitive, but at least it works. Originally designed in 1998, TarotSchool.com has grown to be quite extensive. An updated design is currently on our long-term "To Do" list.

Launching your own website? Work with an experienced web designer if you have the opportunity, but also take the time to learn as much as you can so that you don't need to depend on someone else to do your updates. These days, there are some wonderful programs that will help you create an integrated professional look. There's also a tremendous amount of information and advice online to guide you through the process.

Bonus Tips

- Websites are most successful if their content changes regularly; if you choose to have one, get professional advice when designing it, but learn to update it yourself

- Keep it active and interesting to readers, giving them a reason to come back

Tarot Tips

As part of our internet presence, we began publishing a weekly email newsletter in October, 1998. Called "Tarot Tips," it started out as (and was supposed to remain) a very short weekly tip of a paragraph or two on a practical reading technique. It didn't stay that way for long, as you can see by the material in this book. The tips got longer, and many additional resources were added as well. Eventually, time constraints made it impossible to keep up the weekly schedule, but we still publish an issue whenever we can.

An email newsletter is an excellent way to keep your name in front of the public. Whether your content is purely informational, or you use it as a vehicle to help market your classes or services, it is a quick and economical way to reach a large group of people. (Patience Alert: building your list does take time.)

With the huge amount of email that most people get these days, a monthly schedule is probably best. If you need to communicate more frequently, a weekly or bi-weekly publication is fine, but spare your public a daily newsletter unless you know for sure that's what they want. If you already have a list, and are considering changing your publishing schedule, take a poll of your readers to see which frequency they prefer.

Bonus Tips

- Make use of available communication vehicles; e-mail is a great way to keep in touch with students or clients on a regular basis

Hold the Phone!

Late that same year, we learned of a relatively new technology called the telebridge that was being used extensively in the Personal Coaching industry. It allowed thirty, fifty, or even 100 people to call in to a central phone number and participate in a conference call which they called a "teleclass." Although the conference call wasn't a new idea, telebridge technology made the calls much easier and more affordable than they had been. Here was a new way that we could teach people outside of New York.

Teaching over the telephone required a new set of skills, so we took a series of courses in Teleclass Leader Training. Armed with these new techniques, we began offering Tarot Teleclasses in January, 1999.

As with our live classes, the content and format of our teleclasses and telecourses has varied over the years. We've used them to present material that doesn't fit into the format of our weekly divination skills class. All the teleclasses are taped, which enables us to continue to offer them to the public while we develop new courses.

We discovered that phone classes are focused and intimate, and our teleclass students, who come from all over the country, have formed a remarkably bonded group energy.

The dynamics of teaching on the phone are different from teaching a live class. If you'd like to try your hand at offering teleclasses, take the time to get some training—or at the very least, sit in on a number of teleclasses from different teachers to get a sense of their style and technique. An internet search on "teleclasses" should give you plenty of information to get you started.

Bonus Tip

- Keep up on changing technology. Find ways to use it to expand and/or make your work more effective

Our Karmic Surprise

Wald and I met on the Summer Solstice in 1994 and quickly discovered a mutual love of Tarot. When we exchanged our first readings, however, we made a momentous discovery that would pave the way for some of our most creative work. We found that we each had a special way of reading personality that was almost identical. Since then, we have worked together to explore and expand on this method, and we're still making new discoveries about it. To this day, neither of us have ever met anyone else who reads in this way—unless they've learned it from us.

The Elemental Array, the Court Card Personality Array, the Hidden Face, Birth Cards, the Couples Mandala, and the Personal Tree constitute a set of techniques we're continually developing that we call "Tarot Psychology." This has become one of the most important aspects of our work. It does not, as one might assume, combine Tarot with traditional schools of psychology. Rather it describes a unique way of discovering and understanding ourselves as magical beings.

Staying creative is pivotal in maintaining any long-term venture. Our ongoing work with Tarot Psychology has kept us fresh and interested in what we do.

Bonus Tip

- A good teacher is also a good student. Talk with others about their passions, continue learning, and strive for creativity

That's Intense!

When our students began to stay with us longer and longer, we started to look for ways to deepen their knowledge and keep them interested. Thus, the concept of Tarot School Intensives was born.

What distinguishes intensives from our other classes is the length. An intensive is a full-day or weekend learning experience of either eight or sixteen hours. We have found this to be the minimum amount of time needed to introduce in enough depth a special Tarot technique or parallel discipline. The intensive is meant to open a new area of study to our students, or take them much deeper into a topic we've only been able to touch on in shorter classes.

Don't feel you have to teach introductory classes over and over again. Find an aspect of your work that you can explore in depth. If you find it fascinating, so will your students—and they'll thank you for the experience.

Bonus Tips

- As you grow, share with others; after your students master the basics, give them new and exciting ways to apply that knowledge

Roll Tape

At The Tarot School, the thing we love most is a great class. We've had a lot of them, and over the years many of these classes and courses have been taped. In this way, our students never had to miss a class even when they couldn't physically attend, and Tarot lovers too far away to come to live classes or teleclasses could enjoy them from any distance in time or space.

This is how the Tarot School Audio Course Series was born, and over time, slowly but surely, has grown into an extensive collection. It captures on tape the best of our continuous experiments to teach Tarot at the highest level we can personally reach. To maintain the intensity and depth of instruction over the years, we constantly learn, think, and experiment. Classes have evolved into courses, individual techniques have been integrated into practicums, and courses and practicums together have become full, rich studies.

At the beginning, when all these things were taking shape, we had the idea of taping classes so the information they contained wouldn't be lost. Our students loved the idea and began to acquire tapes, creating personal libraries of Tarot instruction. Card study tapes were joined by others on reading technique and special classes in Tarot Psychology, Qabalah, Past Lives, and more. Together, they eventually became an integrated series of audio courses that may already be the most extensive single source of card knowledge and technique in Tarot today.

And it's not just instruction, not just lecture. Every tape enfolds you in the experience of learning, in the warmth and spontaneity of presence in a live and lively class. It's a wonderful way to learn.

Taping your classes is a good idea even if you don't choose to market them to the public. They provide a record of your work, and are a great way to refresh your own memory from time to time, especially if you don't prepare extensive notes.

If you're technologically inclined and have the patience, it's worth taking the time to convert your tapes into digital files and clean up the coughs, stutters and background noise with sound editing software. Once this is done, you can burn them onto CDs for more stable archiving or for CD duplication.

When making copies of your tapes for sale or distribution, you can either send your tapes to a professional duplicating house, or purchase a high-speed duplicator and do it yourself. We use our own duplicator for short runs and outsource larger orders. Professional duplication is more expensive, but it saves us valuable time.

Bonus Tip

- Even if you don't choose to sell tapes of your classes, occasionally tape (or even videotape) your classes; reviewing them is an excellent way to improve your presentation.

Teamwork

Running The Tarot School is our full-time job, and there's no way either one of us could do it alone. We each have different talents, and all our individual skills are constantly called into play. Teamwork is the key ingredient in everything we do, and it helps tremendously that we enjoy each other's company enough to be together 24/7. (We'd really love some extra help and hope to be able to afford that someday.)

Some of our live class students probably think that our job consists entirely of showing up once a week to teach a 3-hour class (with a little extra time allotted to prepare the lesson.) That may have been true when we first started and both had day-jobs, but committing ourselves to The Tarot School full-time changed all that.

There are some things that the two of us do together, and we split the rest of our responsibilities according to our strengths and/or proclivities. Here's a little peek behind-the-scenes:

Research and Development

This is the one area that we share most. We talk with each other all the time and use these discussions to plan events, new classes and courses, and to expand upon our ongoing creative work. We brainstorm, we play; at times we argue—but everything we accomplish results from this lively interchange.

Having someone to bounce ideas off of is not only useful for generating new ideas, but can be a helpful reality check for those times when your enthusiasm starts to get the better of you.

Bonus Tip

- Whether or not you have a partner, make sure you have someone to talk to, to brainstorm with, and to help you develop ideas

Instruction

Wald does most of the talking in our classes but we teach almost all of them together. Our teaching venues include weekly classes in New York City, additional weekly classes at our home, four- to six-week telecourses every month or so, frequent weekend intensives, an occasional retreat, personal telephone coaching sessions, and workshops at Tarot conferences. Our *Tarot Tips* newsletter (and now this book) is another forum for instruction.

If teaching is what you love to do, there are many ways to do it. Think outside the box and you'll find all sorts of opportunities to share what you know.

Bonus Tips

- Look to other teachers for inspiration
- Try techniques that work for others, but give them your own twist
- Try something completely new and different

Reading

We are both constantly reading; it's how we learn, develop new material, and keep in touch with what's happening in the Tarot community. One of us reads books, the other reads a lot of stuff online, and we both read the cards for clients. These days, we like to do what we call "Tandem Tarot" readings, where the two of us read for a single querent. Since we each tend to see different things, this method makes the reading very full.

There is more public access to esoteric information now than ever before. Take advantage of the internet and your local bookstore to keep your mind active and your material fresh. You've probably found that, at one time or another, your card readings make use of everything you've ever learned. Reading is one good way to keep learning.

Bonus Tip

- Keep up with the current works in tarot: new books, new decks, associations, conferences, egroups, and newsletters

Writing

There are many things we do that require writing, and this is another area we share. Although some things end up as a collaboration, much of our writing is done separately. Writing projects include books, articles, correspondence course lessons, telecourse scripts and class notes, newsletters, promotional copy for our website, print advertising and brochures, liner notes for our audio courses, and general correspondence.

If writing doesn't come naturally, consider taking some courses. Or, if you have the resources, hire a good copywriter. Your written material is often the first contact people have with you. Make their first impression a good one!

Bonus Tip

- Writing is important; get an unbiased, knowledgeable opinion; hire a professional rather than present unprofessional materials

Arithmetic

Running any business involves working with numbers. Wald handles numbers better so he gets to balance the checkbook, do the banking, and take care of our general accounting. He also keeps track of our class attendance records. Ruth Ann gets to play with the credit card machine and keep records of product orders and class registrations. We both frequently calculate Tarot birth card combinations for our students and reading clients as well.

"One . . . Two . . . Few . . . Many . . . ." If your facility with numbers has carried over from a past life in the Dark Ages, be sure to check all your calculations at least twice, and hire a good accountant to prepare your taxes!

Bonus Tips

- Keep accurate and extensive records
- Retain the services of a good accountant

Technology

This is another place where we have distinct talents and responsibilities. Ruth Ann is the resident techie and does everything that involves the computer: all layout and design, database management, email, typing (see Writing), and internet-based research. She is also our webmistress and does the digital conversion and sound editing of our audio courses. Wald handles the tape recording and in-house duplication work. We both rely on our friend David to maintain our computer, save us when things go wrong with the hardware or software, and to help with those inevitable learning curves.

Even if you were born with a computer mouse in your hand, there are going to be times when having some technical support is crucial. Who do you know who knows more than you do?

Bonus Tip

- Develop a strong network of reliable service professionals, from copywriting to accounting to web design to technological support

Shopping

You have to spend money to make money, and The Tarot School is no exception. We have to buy all sorts of things. Here's a sample of our shopping list:

Books for resale and research

Postage and office supplies

Printing

Advertising space

Special event goods and services

Technical equipment

Educational opportunities

Tarot School logo merchandise (Tarot bags, tote bags, t-
shirts, etc.)

Car and travel

Telephone and internet expenses

. . . and a whole range of miscellaneous purchases that can't
be categorized.

Any business is full of hidden costs. If you're just starting out,
make sure to budget money for mystery expenses—you'll soon
discover you have needs you didn't anticipate. Keeping a careful
record of your spending is always a good idea. Money tends to slip
between the cracks when you're not paying attention.

Bonus Tips

- Write down every expenditure
- Revise your budget as your gain a more realistic knowledge of expenses

Fulfillment

Running The Tarot School is very fulfilling work—and we spend
a lot of time doing fulfillment! Getting orders is great, but we find
getting them out is hard work. This is one of those places we sure
wish we had some help. Once payment for an order has been
processed and it's been entered into the database, the fulfillment
phase begins.

First you must make sure you have adequate inventory on
hand. You'll also need packaging and postage (check those postal

rates!). Label your packages clearly and weigh them with a good electronic postal scale. A tenth of an ounce can make a difference in the shipping rate, and you don't want your packages returned for lack of proper postage. (We've learned this the hard way.)

As simple as this sounds, order fulfillment can be very time consuming. The more successful you are, the more time you'll have to allot for this task. And if you're working by yourself, that can be an important consideration. This is another job we share as much as possible.

Bonus Tip

- Whether it's a product or service, make sure you deliver what you promise

Depending on the direction of your Tarot business, you may or may not need to work so closely with a partner. But if you do, divvy up your responsibilities according to your strengths, and find ways to work in parallel so you're not in each other's face all the time. That way, when you do collaborate on a project, your conversations can be filled with energy, not bickering.

Dinner and a Movie

We rarely get to take a week-long vacation from our busy work schedule, but we make sure to schedule in lots of "vacation" time in order to keep our sanity. We do this by eating out and/or going to the movies.

A movie is a great way to switch gears and give your brain a rest. Even though we'll sometimes rent a movie or watch one on television, we prefer to see them on the big screen. It's more exciting and mentally involving, and there aren't the usual distractions of home such a ringing phone. We do much of our work from home, and going to the movie theater gets us out of the house.

We take these two to three hour vacations at least once a week. If we can, we'll see two movies—and sometimes even three! In the long run, it's less expensive than going on a real vacation, and we get to stretch out the fun all year long.

This also gives us something to talk about besides Tarot!

Bonus Tips

- Make sure you take breaks from your work

- Be creative: find inexpensive and enjoyable ways to spend your time off

- Maintain your other interests; don't let your business take over your life and become who you are; maintaining other interests and hobbies makes you a more interesting, balanced, and healthy individual

Degrees of Change

When you've put in the time and effort that in-depth study requires, it's nice to have something to show for it. We grant students an internal degree for the equivalent of a year's study in any of a number of our programs. But although a Tarot School degree does recognize students for their work and dedication, the philosophy behind our degree program goes beyond simple recognition.

As we see it, there are three kinds of degree. The most familiar is the academic degree that is granted by educational institutions. The second type is the initiatory degree that is common to spiritual paths such as Wicca or Freemasonry. A Tarot School degree is meant to measure the degree of change a student experiences after a year's worth of study. This degree of change is personal, and therefore different for everyone—but it's tangible, and something we as teachers can vouch for.

Our degrees are cumulative. You can earn a Third Degree, for instance, by taking a year's worth of Divination Skills classes, 100 hours of teleclasses, and completing our Correspondence Course Degree Program. Or double up on any single course of study for a Second Degree. The more degrees you have, the more change we've witnessed.

It took us a bit of trial and error to develop and define our degree program. It works very well with our varied curriculum, but you don't need to offer anything quite so elaborate. Even if you're only teaching a one-day workshop, giving your students a Certificate of Completion is a validation of the work they've done, and proof of professional study if they should ever need it.

Bonus Tips
- Give your students something to take away, some evidence of their investment

Heart to Heart

There's a bit of common wisdom that says, "a strong business is built one relationship at a time." We take that sentiment very seriously, and spend as much time as possible giving our students, colleagues, and customers our personal attention. As we grow, it becomes more difficult to do this consistently, but we do the best we can.

Wald spends a good part of each day on the phone, talking with our students and other Tarot professionals. For people enrolled in our correspondence course degree program, he'll spend many hours every month reviewing lesson submissions and conducting one-on-one coaching sessions.

Communication by phone serves a number of other functions as well. Long experience has taught us that standard forms of advertising, marketing and promotion are not cost-effective, at least in our case. When we do mailings, the response we get has never yet paid for the out-of-pocket expense, not to mention the time and effort each mailing takes. And advertising in magazines and newspapers has barely paid for itself—and in some cases costs us more than it brings in. For us, our website does a much better job at this kind of promotion.

We have found that personal contact and friendly conversation with our current and potential students and customers is far and away the most effective way to let people know what we're doing at any given time. This also gives us a chance to find out what's going on with them, address any problems they may have with an order, listen to their suggestions for future Tarot School projects, and in general, keep the channels of communication wide open.

It has become an important part of the way we do business to treat others with love and respect. We truly appreciate those who take an interest in our work, and have formed very special relationships with numerous students and colleagues as a result of taking a heart-centered approach.

Bonus Tips

- Treat all your students and/or clients with professionalism and respect
- Determine which modes of advertising are the most effective for your business

Love Story

At one of the conferences hosted by the American Tarot Association, we were encouraged to produce an event on the East Coast. Except for a small symposium held earlier in Boca Raton, Florida, all of the Tarot conferences had been held in California and the Midwest. Our previous event-planning experience was limited to small intensives, workshops, and retreats, but we decided we were ready for the challenge. We began the four-year planning process for the New York Tarot Festival.

All this time, our relationship had been growing stronger. Two years later, as the century turned, we became engaged.

So now we would be planning two events—the festival and our wedding! At some point, it occurred to us to combine them. This way, our colleagues who were flying in for the Tarot Festival could also attend the wedding. At first we thought we'd have a quiet ceremony in one of the hotel conference rooms, or maybe even sneak off to the park. But as time went on, our plans became more and more elaborate. Ultimately, we took up three sections of the Grand Ballroom and invited all the festival participants (more than 200 people), plus family and friends, to witness our vows.

Robert Moyer designed and created our elaborate wedding garb, as well as a magical setting for the ceremony—complete with hanging banners of the Four Aces, a beautiful altar, a grove of trees, and a black-and-white checkered floor! Lon Milo DuQuette and Mary K. Greer were our real-life Hierophant and High Priestess, and a group of family and friends rounded out the wedding party. The ceremony, which we wrote ourselves (in our spare time!), was filled with Tarot symbolism and other personal spiritual references. Mince Pye put the icing on the cake with beautiful Renaissance music, and a good time was had by all.

The New York Tarot Festival itself, which was held during the weekend of June 21–23, 2002, was a whirlwind of classes taught by a dozen of the best Tarot instructors around. We specifically requested that everyone present a hands-on workshop instead of a lecture, and the participants were delighted with the experience. There were rituals, parties, an evening in Manhattan, and a Merchants Faire for shopping.

Thinking back on it now, we can't imagine how we managed all the details. We couldn't have pulled it off at all without the help of Lelia and Irene, and a dedicated crew of friends, family, and volunteers from the Tarot School student body. The financial risk was tremendous, and the anxiety level bordered on soul-shattering. But we were blessed, and with the help of a last-minute article in *The Village Voice* which resulted in a flurry of walk-in registrations, we just about broke even.

We attempted an event of that size because we were innocent. We succeeded through hard work and grace. The best advice we can offer if you want to produce a public event of any size is to Take… Your… Time…. Our plans must have gone through at least a half-dozen incarnations before they were realized, and we re-negotiated the contract with the hotel four times. But when it was finally showtime, we knew what we wanted, and we knew what we were doing.

Bonus Tips

- Don't be afraid to try something big

- Another reason to have a large network: Learn from others' experiences

The Readers Studio

Shortly afterward, the let-down hit. We were so used to working at a furious rate, our regular projects seemed almost boring by comparison. The community wanted us to do another event, and even though we had been swearing up, down and sideways that we would never do anything like that again, we were hooked!

We weren't, however, hubristic enough to tempt the gods by planning another event of that magnitude. We decided to do something more intimate, yet we wanted it to be special—something that had never been done before.

After giving it a good deal of thought, we realized that what was missing from the Tarot event calendar was a conference expressly designed for professional readers and teachers. The

Readers Studio was created not only to serve the needs of more experienced Tarotists, but to give instructors a rare opportunity to teach at their highest level.

The first Readers Studio, coproduced by Llewellyn Worldwide, was held in April, 2003. Attendance was capped at seventy-eight seats and three top-notch teachers, Rachel Pollack, Mary Greer and Nina Lee Braden, presented four-hour practical workshops geared to raising everyone's reading skills to the next level. The format was simpler than the festival's but the feedback we received was very positive, and we plan to make it an annual event.

Bonus Tip

- Shoot for the stars! In less than ten years, the Tarot School went from having a few students to teaching hundreds of people from all over the world. They host large-scale, successful events featuring some of the most exciting names in Tarot. Where will you be in ten years? Imagine the possibilities, learn as much as possible, roll up your sleeves, and see what happens.

Predicting the Future …

The evolution of The Tarot School has been organic, and we really can't predict its future. We'll keep teaching, of course, and we'd like to write more books. We'll continue the programs we have in place, but new directions always come as a surprise. We look forward to discovering what those new directions will be, and to sharing the adventure of Tarot with you!

— Ruth Ann and Wald Amberstone

To Write to the Authors

If you wish to contact the authors or would like more information about this book, please write to the authors in care of Llewellyn Worldwide and we will forward your request. Both the authors and publisher appreciate hearing from you and learning of your enjoyment of this book. Llewellyn Worldwide cannot guarantee that every letter written to the author will be answered, but all will be forwarded. Please write to:

Wald & Ruth Ann Amberstone
c/o Llewellyn Worldwide
P.O. Box 64383, Dept. 0-7387-0216-1
St. Paul, MN 55164-0383, U.S.A.
Please include a self-addressed, stamped envelope with your letter. If outside the U.S.A., enclose international postal coupons.

Many of Llewellyn's authors have websites with additional information and resources. For more information, please visit our website at www.llewellyn.com.

Index

drawing a blank, 74, 101, 144

Earth Signs, 80
Element, 31, 45–46, 49, 55,
    80–81, 162
esoteric correspondence, 82
esoteric function, 38, 52, 83
evening, 77, 160, 182

Faery Wicca, 25
fan, 71
fear, 68, 126, 131
fee, 148
feedback, 28, 35, 69–70, 74, 161,
    165, 183
feminist, 15, 29, 32
Fertility & Barrenness, 83
Fire, 31–32, 42, 45–46, 80, 83,
    87, 95
Fire Signs, 80
Functions, 52, 56, 73, 82–83, 180
future, 23, 60–61, 77–78, 88–89,
    151–153, 180, 184

gay, 14–15
Gemini, 53, 79–80, 83
gift, 1–2, 114, 162, 207
Golden Dawn, 32, 74, 82,
    156–157

health readings, 50, 208
Hearing, 83, 185
honest dealings, 146

imagery, 16–17, 23, 31–32, 50,
    52, 100, 126, 157, 165, 207
imagination, 83, 140
Indignation & Grace, 83

interpretation, 5, 7, 19–31, 33,
    35, 37, 39, 41–43, 45, 47, 49,
    51, 53, 55, 57, 73–76, 85, 89,
    92, 100–102, 104, 106, 138,
    157
intuition, xii,10, 16, 26, 28, 32,
    40, 43, 45, 52, 73, 76–77, 93,
    111
intuitive interpretations, 25, 33,
    52

journal, 6, 95, 144, 162
Judgement, 54, 56, 64, 83, 130
Justice, 53–54, 64, 79, 83,
    129–130
King of Pentacles, 36, 40
King of Wands, 42, 51
knowledge, xi–xii, xv–xvi,
    19–20, 27, 35–36, 42, 49–50,
    52, 55, 59–60, 66–67, 76,
    79–80, 93, 105, 124–125,
    135–136, 147, 169–171, 176

laughter, 38, 83
layouts, 115–117, 145
Leo, 53, 79–81, 83
levels of interpretation, 33
Libra, 53, 79–80, 83
Life & Death, 28, 36–38, 40, 50,
    53–54, 56, 68, 75, 79, 83, 86,
    90, 92–93, 95, 121, 130–131,
    135, 137–138, 141–143
limits of expertise, 146
LWB, 24
Major Arcana, 34, 52, 57, 82,
    109, 112, 129, 165
Majors, 34, 78, 86–87
manifesting, 45, 132

ORDER LLEWELLYN BOOKS TODAY!

Llewellyn publishes hundreds of books on your favorite subjects! To get these exciting books, including the ones on the following pages, check your local bookstore or order them directly from Llewellyn.

Order Online:

Visit our website at www.llewellyn.com, select your books, and order them on our secure server.

Order by Phone:

- Call toll-free within the U.S. at 1-877-NEW-WRLD (1-877-639-9753)
  Call toll-free within Canada at 1-866-NEW-WRLD (1-866-639-9753)
- We accept VISA, MasterCard, and American Express

Order by Mail:

Send the full price of your order (MN residents add 7% sales tax) in U.S. funds, plus postage & handling to:

Llewellyn Worldwide
P.O. Box 64383, Dept. 0-7387-0216-1
St. Paul, MN 55164-0383, U.S.A.

Postage & Handling:

Standard (U.S., Mexico, & Canada). If your order is:

Up to $25.00, add $3.50
$25.01 - $48.99, add $4.00
$49.00 and over, FREE STANDARD SHIPPING

(Continental U.S. orders ship UPS. AK, HI, PR, & P.O. Boxes ship USPS 1st class. Mex. & Can. ship PMB.)

International Orders:

Surface Mail: For orders of $20.00 or less, add $5 plus $1 per item ordered. For orders of $20.01 and over, add $6 plus $1 per item ordered.

Air Mail:

Books: Postage & Handling is equal to the total retail price of all books in the order.
Non-book items: Add $5 for each item.

Orders are processed within 2 business days. Please allow for normal shipping time.
Postage and handling rates subject to change.

Tarot for Self-Discovery

Foreword by Mary K. Greer
Nina Lee Braden

The cards have a message for you!

Tarot cards can be extremely useful in helping us to decipher the messages from our subconscious, since the pictures on the cards "speak" the language of the subconscious—the language of symbols and pictures and imagination. *Tarot for Self-Discovery* is not about learning the Tarot per se; rather it is a book of 47 exercises that will help you use the Tarot cards for personal and spiritual growth. Whether you need help going through a difficult transition in your life, or you want to know the next step on your path, the images on the cards contain messages exclusively for you.

- Contains 47 Tarot exercises for every purpose, including improving relationships and meeting your guardian angel, to healing grief and finding your life purpose

- The exercises personalize the cards for each reader, so they become portals for deeper understanding of the self

- The exercises narrow down the immense data contained in the cards into an experience that is remembered

- For beginners or advanced Tarot readers

- For use with any Tarot deck

0-7387-0170-X, 6 x 9, 168 pp.   **$12.95**

The Complete book of Tarot Reversals

Mary K. Greer

*The topsy-turvy world of
upside-down cards*

What do you do with the "other half" of a Tarot reading: the reversed cards? Just ignore them as many people do? Tarot Reversals reveals everything you need to know for reading the most maligned and misunderstood part of a spread. These interpretations offer inner support, positive advice, and descriptions of the learning opportunities available, yet with a twist that is uniquely their own.

Enhance and deepen the quality of your consultations as you experiment with the eleven different methods of reading reversed cards. Use the author's interpretations to stimulate your own intuitive ideas. Struggle in the dark no longer.

This is the first book to fully and exclusively address the interpretation of cards that appear upside-down in a Tarot spread. It features eleven different methods of determining reversed card meanings.

1-56718-285-2, 6 x 9, 312 pp.   **$14.95**

Designing Your Own Tarot Spreads

Foreword by Mary K. Greer
Teresa Michelsen

Tailor your spreads to the questions
your clients ask everyday

Handle every topic with confidence and clarity as you learn to design readings that really answer the question asked. Why rely on the Celtic Cross or Past-Present-Future spread when you can develop layouts that reflect your personal style and your client's concerns?

This book covers all the fundamentals of spread design with examples and exercises. Get inspirations for spreads covering a wide variety of topics. Learn how to frame the question; how many cards to use; the meanings of each card position; working with reversals and dignities; and how to use special cards such as significators, clarification cards, and karmic lesson cards.

Topics include relationships, financial and career development, predictive readings, timing readings, personal development, spiritual readings, and special occasion spreads.

ISBN 0-7387-0263-3, 6 x 9, 192 pp.,   **$12.95**